generations
TOGETHER

Favorite Recipes from

SISTERHOOD OF AGUDATH ISRAEL ✡ ETZ AHAYEM SYNAGOGUE
MONTGOMERY, ALABAMA

Generations Eat Together

ISBN: 978-0-615-70543-9
January 2013   First printing 1500 copies

Copies of **Generations Eat Together** may be obtained by sending $25.00 plus $8.00 for shipping, handling and sales tax to:

Sisterhood of Agudath Israel ✡ Etz Ahayem
3525 Cloverdale Road
Montgomery Alabama 36111

334-281-7394

These recipes represent our Eastern European and Mediterranean roots, as well as family favorites influenced by tastes from the new South, the old South and other places. Through the years, they have been tried, tested, adapted and definitely altered by the cooks who have prepared them, shared them and passed them down. Therefore, no claim is made that these are all original recipes.

Cover Artist: Karla Merritt
Drawings Artist: Jeff Preg

Printed in USA by

WIMMER
cookbooks
A CONSOLIDATED GRAPHICS COMPANY
wimmerco.com   800.548.2537

Thank you for making this happen!

Cookbook Committee for **Generations Eat Together**

Co Chairpersons — Jo Anne H. Rousso and Anita L. Capouano

Our Sisterhood's dream of a congregational cookbook would not have been possible without the tireless efforts of the Cookbook Committee. From editing to proofing to keying in the recipes, these members gave countless hours of time to make **Generations Eat Together** a reality. We appreciate their efforts and praise their commitment. A special thanks to.....

Emily Allen	Dale Evans	Esther Miller
Lani Ashner	Pearl Hasson	Marsha Orange
Rhonda Blitz	Karen Herman	Lanie Raymon
Diane Blondheim	Kathy Hess	Jeanette Rousso
Joy Blondheim	Phyllis Kasover	Fern Shinbaum
Sylvia Capouano	Elaine Kirkpatrick	Bella Smith
Kathie Cohen	Irene Kramer	Rebecca Ternus
Mae Cohen	Bonnie Labovitz	

Linda Simonds, Synagogue Office Manager

Generations Eat Together is partially funded by a donation made in memory of Ruth and Morris Segall.

Introduction

*I*n Jewish families, regardless of whether they are secular or deeply religious, they share one important emotion...a passion for foods. Gathering around a table laden with fresh, delicious, home-cooked favorites is a mainstay of family life. Cooking and enjoying food together are a part of the fabric of our lives, bound together like the dough in our classic breads.

Generations Eat Together is a collection of personal recipes from the members of Agudath Israel ✡ Etz Ahayem Synagogue. Within these pages, each recipe reflects the tapestry of foods that has been woven into the lives of grandmothers, mothers and granddaughters for over 500 years.

Both the Ashkenazi women from Eastern Europe and the Sephardic women from the island of Rhodes in the Mediterranean passed down much loved recipes that create feasts for the palate from their different cultures. Add to this traditional fare, contemporary favorites, often with a Southern flare, and you have an extraordinary culinary combination awaiting you.

The emphasis is on an abundance of sharing and the special feeling that comes with enjoying good food with family and people you love.

AGUDATH ISRAEL ✡ ETZ AHAYEM
Sisterhood

Since its beginning in 1906 as Agudath Israel's Ladies Hebrew Charity Society and in 1919 as Etz Ahayem's Sisterhood, the Sisterhood of Agudath Israel ✡ Etz Ahayem is the organization that has been the backbone of our Synagogue. Sisterhood has helped us maintain our Jewish identity, value our heritage, celebrate Jewish life and deepen our love for synagogue and faith. With this publication, Sisterhood has permanently etched the foods we love into history... so generations eat together... lovingly and forever.

Welcome to our house and to our table. Every Jewish meal begins with this blessing that is recited while holding a piece of bread.

Barukh ata Adonai, Eloheinu melekh ha'olam, hamotzi lehem min ha'aretz
Blessed are You, Lord our God, Ruler of the universe, who brings forth bread from the earth.

Table of Contents

Starters...

...that Generations Eat Together!

Appetizers

Soups

Salads

Pickling

Whether it's a family meal or a dinner party with friends,
the starters you serve set the mood for mingling and conversations.
We are pleased to share some of our favorites. They are sure
to have your family and guests talking...and get your
meal started on a delicious note!

Cheese Wafers

1	cup grated sharp cheese	1½	cups crispy rice cereal
½	cup margarine or butter	1½	teaspoons cayenne pepper, or
1	cup flour		to taste

Preheat oven to 350°. Put cheese into large bowl. Melt margarine or butter; pour over cheese. Add flour. Mix well. Add cereal and pepper. Mix well. Roll into marble sized pieces; flatten. Bake on cookie sheet 10-13 minutes.

DAIRY *Phyllis Kasover*

Baked Goat Cheese in Tomato-Olive Oil Sauce

1	tablespoon extra virgin olive oil	1	thin baguette, thinly sliced or bruschetta from market
2	large garlic cloves, minced		
1	(16 ounce) can crushed tomatoes	1	(about 10 ounces) log goat cheese, sliced crosswise, ¼-inch thick
8-10	black olives, sliced		

Preheat oven to 450°. Place oil and garlic in Dutch oven; cook on medium heat until garlic starts to sizzle and turn golden. Add tomatoes and olives; lower to simmer; cook until sauce is thick, 10-13 minutes. Remove garlic. Place bread rounds in single layer on oven rack set in center position. Bake until golden, about 5 minutes. Put tomato sauce into 9-inch ovenproof pan; top with goat cheese discs. Bake until bubbly, about 10 minutes. Turn on broil; cook until goat cheese is lightly brown, 1 or 2 minutes. Serve with toasts.

Sauce can be covered and refrigerated up to 5 days. Return to room temperature before heating.

DAIRY *Corinne F. Capilouto*

Arline Miller's Cheese Ball

2   tablespoons minced green
    onions
2   (8 ounce) packages Philadelphia
    cream cheese
2   (8 ounce) cans crushed
    pineapple, drained

¼   cup chopped bell pepper
    Season salt to taste
1   cup chopped pecans, divided

Mix onions, cream cheese, pineapple, bell pepper, season salt and ½ cup
pecans. Form into 1 large or 2 small cheese balls. Roll in remaining ½ cup
pecans. Wrap in plastic wrap; refrigerate until ready to serve.

DAIRY   *Rita Rosenthal*

Curry Cheese Ball

2   (8 ounce) packages cream
    cheese
½   cup chutney
2   teaspoons curry powder

½   teaspoon dry mustard
¼   teaspoon ginger
½   cup almond slices, toasted

Soften cream cheese. Add chutney, curry powder, mustard and ginger. Stir
until all ingredients are blended together. Spread almonds on foil or wax paper.
Spoon cheese on top of almonds, shaping into a ball; press remaining almonds
into top and sides of cheese ball to cover completely.

DAIRY   *Marsha Orange*

Golden Cheese Squares

2	cups Bisquick	$\frac{1}{2}$	cup butter
$1\frac{1}{2}$	teaspoons baking powder	$2\frac{1}{2}$	cups feta cheese
$\frac{1}{4}$	teaspoon salt	1	cup small-curd cottage cheese
1	cup milk	3	large eggs, slightly beaten

Preheat oven to 350°. Stir Bisquick, baking powder, salt, milk, butter, cheeses and eggs just until dry ingredients are moistened. Place cheese mixture in lightly greased 15x10 jelly-roll pan. Bake 30 minutes or until lightly brown and set. Remove from oven; cool on rack 10 minutes. Cut into squares.

Freezes well.

Makes about 60 squares

DAIRY   *Sandi Stern*

Ajada — Potato and Garlic Dip

4	white potatoes	1	cup fresh lemon juice
2	eggs	1	teaspoon salt
2	cloves garlic, crushed	$\frac{1}{4}$	cup olive oil

Peel and boil potatoes; rice or mash fine. Measure out 3 cups potatoes. Reserve remainder for future use. While potatoes are still very hot, add eggs. Mix well. Gradually add garlic, lemon juice, salt and oil. Beat until slightly thicker than mayonnaise. Chill. Serve with crackers or pita points.

Serves 12 to 16

PARVE   *Sephardic Dinner 2007*

Lois' Cheese Beignets

canola oil for deep frying

¼ cup unsalted butter

1 cup water

1 cup flour

4 eggs

¾ teaspoon salt

½ teaspoon dry mustard

1 teaspoon Dijon mustard

1¼ cups grated sharp Cheddar cheese

Heat oil in a deep fryer, following manufacturer's instructions. In saucepan, bring butter and water to boil. Remove from heat. Stir in flour; mix to form a loose ball. Cool. Place dough in food processor fitted with steel cutting blade. Add eggs one at a time; process after each addition. Add salt, mustards; process. Add cheese; process. Drop mixture by rounded teaspoons into hot oil, being careful not to overload fryer. When brown, remove with a slotted spoon; drain on paper towels. Use immediately or freeze individually on cookie sheet; place in a plastic bag when frozen. Defrost as needed; crisp in 350° oven.

Makes about 50

DAIRY   *Toby Gewant*

Berenjena — Eggplant Spread

2 large eggplants

2 teaspoons salt

2 tablespoons oil

Juice of 1 lemon

2 cloves garlic or 1 chopped onion

Hot sauce or hot peppers to taste, optional

Preheat oven to 400°. Pierce skin of eggplants with fork; bake until soft and skin is shriveled. Cool enough to remove skin. Chop up pulp; add salt, oil, lemon juice, garlic or onion and hot sauce or peppers, if using. Mix well. Chill. Serve with pita crackers.

PARVE   *Sephardic Dinner 2007*

Greek Layered Dip

1   cup plain hummus
¾   cup Greek fat-free plain yogurt
1   teaspoon chopped parsley
1   teaspoon lemon juice
⅛   teaspoon pepper
1   tomato, seeded, chopped

⅓   cup chopped cucumber
¼   cup chopped scallions
½   cup crumbled feta cheese
    Sliced cucumber, various colored bell pepper slices and Kalamata olives for garnish

Spread hummus on large platter. Mix yogurt with parsley, lemon juice and pepper. Spread over hummus. Dry tomato and cucumber on paper towels to remove all excess moisture; spread over hummus. Mix scallions and feta cheese; layer over tomatoes and cucumbers. Garnish with bell peppers, cucumber and olives.

DAIRY   *Sandi Stern*

Freida's Ugly Dip

1   (11 ounce) can white shoepeg corn, drained
1   (15.5 ounce) can black beans, rinsed, drained
1   (4 ounce) package crumbled feta cheese
1   small bunch green onions, chopped

½   cup extra-light olive oil
½   cup sugar
½   cup apple cider vinegar
    Garlic powder to taste
    Salt to taste
    Pepper to taste
    Corn chip scoops

Combine corn, black beans, feta cheese and green onions; refrigerate. Combine oil, sugar, vinegar, garlic powder, salt and pepper in food processor or dressing shaker. Refrigerate 1 hour before serving. Pour as much dressing as you like over vegetable mixture; toss well. Save unused dressing for future use. Return to refrigerator until ready to serve. Serve with corn chip scoops.

Serves 6 to 8

DAIRY   *Marsha Orange*

Chopped Eggplant by Esther S. Labovitz

1   large eggplant
    Salt to taste
    Pepper to taste
1/2 cup chopped onion

Juice of 1/2 lemon
2   tablespoons olive oil or
    mayonnaise

Pierce eggplant; cook in microwave until soft. Let eggplant cool, peel and mash; put 1 cup in bowl. Add salt, pepper, onion, lemon juice and oil. Stir to mix all. Serve cold with crackers.

__PARVE__   *Betty Ehrlich & Elaine Kirkpatrick*

Spinach Stuffed Mushrooms

2   tablespoons olive oil
2   (8 ounce) packages large,
    stuffing-size white mushrooms
1/2 cup chopped onion
1   teaspoon salt
2   teaspoons pepper

3   cloves garlic, minced
1   (5 ounce) package fresh baby
    spinach, chopped
1/2 cup shredded low-moisture part-
    skim mozzarella cheese
1/4 cup shredded Parmesan cheese

Preheat oven to 350°. Line baking pan with aluminum foil; spray with cooking spray. Clean mushrooms; remove and mince stems. In large skillet sauté onions and mushroom stems. Add salt, pepper and garlic; sauté 1 minute. Lower heat to low; add spinach. Cook until spinach is heated through. Add mozzarella cheese; cook until cheese is melted and all ingredients are well blended. Don't overcook. Spinach should appear wilted, but not "mushy". Remove from heat. Stuff mushroom caps generously with spinach mixture. Place on cookie sheet, filling side up; top each one with Parmesan cheese. Bake 30 minutes or until mushrooms are soft and darker in color.

Serves 8 to 12

__DAIRY__   *Jo Anne H. Rousso*

Lynne's Jalapeño Corn Dip

½ cup unsalted butter

1½ (8 ounce) packages cream
     cheese, nonfat works just fine

1 large sweet onion, chopped

3-4 (15 ounce) cans shoepeg corn

1¾ cups whipping cream

Chopped jalapeño peppers,
     drained, liquid reserved

Liquid from peppers,
     1-2 tablespoons, according
     to preference

Preheat oven to 350°. Melt butter and cream cheese in microwave; stir
together. Add chopped onion, corn, whipping cream, jalapeño peppers and
pepper juice. Mix well. Place in 9x13 dish. Bake 30 minutes or until lightly
browned on top. Serve with corn chips or scoops.

*Refrigerate unused portion; reheats well. For deeper flavor, combine the day
before and refrigerate. You may vary ingredient amounts fairly easily — more
onions, more corn, more heat.*

DAIRY   *Karen Herman*

Tahini Dip

½ cup tahini

1 garlic clove, finely chopped or
     crushed

½ small onion, finely chopped or
     crushed

¼ cup water

Juice of 1 lemon

½ teaspoon cumin powder

Salt to taste

Pepper to taste

½ cup chopped parsley, optional

Combine tahini, garlic, onion and water in bowl; mix well. Add lemon juice,
cumin, salt and pepper. Mixture should be creamy. If too thick, add a little more
water. Cover; refrigerate at least 1 hour. Just before serving, if using, sprinkle
parsley on top of dip. Serve with crackers of your choice.

Makes 1½ cups

PARVE   *Gaby Capp*

Tapenade Olive Spread

2   cloves garlic, minced

8   ounces pitted Kalamata olives, rinsed in cold water, dried on paper towel

4   ounces roasted red peppers, dried on paper towel

1   tablespoon capers, rinsed and drained

2   tablespoons extra virgin olive oil

1½ teaspoons fresh lemon juice

1   tablespoon fresh parsley
    Pepper to taste

Place garlic in processor; process until fine. Add olives, peppers, capers, olive oil, lemon juice, parsley and pepper. Process 1 minute. Mixture should be coarsely chopped. Transfer to bowl; serve with pita chips or crackers.

Can be refrigerated up to 2 weeks.

PARVE   *Corinne F. Capilouto*

Palamida — Pickled Fish Appetizer

2   pounds fresh king mackerel or salmon fillets

¼   cup salt, approximately

Vegetable oil
Fresh lemon and/or orange juice

Coat shallow glass pan with thin layer of plain salt; set aside. Rinse and remove skin from fish. Cut into palm-of-your-hand size pieces. Place fish flat in a single layer in prepared dish. Sprinkle salt liberally on top of fish. Cover with plastic wrap. Place weight such as canned goods or heavy pottery dish on top of plastic wrap. Cover all with foil. Refrigerate 2-3 days. Each day drain off water that accumulates in bottom of pan. On day 3 fish should be firm. If not, drain off water; allow another day. Remove fish, cut into 1-inch pieces. Pack tightly in glass jars; cover with vegetable oil. Refrigerate. When ready to serve, place fish on serving dish. Cover generously with fresh lemon and/or orange juice.

PARVE   *Sephardic Dinner 2007*

Curried Beef Strips

½ cup soy sauce
1 cup good quality olive oil
¼ cup vinegar
2 cups cooked rib steak, cut into
     julienne strips
1 medium onion, sliced thin

½ stalk celery, sliced thin
1 tablespoon peppercorns
½ cup mayonnaise
1 teaspoon curry powder
     Pinch dry mustard, optional

Mix soy sauce, oil and vinegar in shallow mixing bowl. Add strips of beef; stir, making sure all of meat is covered in liquid. Stir in onion and celery; sprinkle with peppercorns. Cover; marinate 8 hours in refrigerator, stirring several times. Before serving, combine mayonnaise, curry powder and mustard powder, if using. Drain meat in colander. Do not pat dry. Toss meat with curried mayonnaise; serve with toothpicks and snack bread.

Serves 8

MEAT   Toby Gewant

Sophie Kulbersh's Sweet and Sour Meatballs

2 pounds ground beef
1 egg, slightly beaten
1 large onion, chopped
     Salt to taste

¼ cup oil
1 (12 ounce) bottle chili sauce
     Juice of 1 lemon
1 cup grape jelly

Combine beef, egg, onion and salt; mix; shape into small balls. Place in single layer in skillet or Dutch oven; brown in oil. Remove; drain meatballs. Wipe excess oil from pan. Return meatballs to pan. Mix chili sauce, lemon juice and jelly. Pour over meatballs. Cover; simmer until thoroughly heated. Serve hot.

MEAT   Rita Rosenthal

Yalangi — Grape Leaves Stuffed with Rice

2	medium onions, chopped
1/2	green bell pepper, chopped
1	cup chopped celery, stalks and leaves
7	tablespoons oil, divided
1	cup rice, rinsed, drained
2	medium tomatoes, peeled, chopped

1 1/2	teaspoons salt
1/2	teaspoon pepper
2 1/4	cups water, divided
	Juice of 2 lemons, divided
1/2	teaspoon dried dill
2	tablespoons chopped parsley
1	(1 pound) jar grapevine leaves, rinsed, drained

Sauté onions, bell pepper and celery in 4 tablespoons oil; add rice, tomatoes, salt, pepper and 3/4 cup water. Cover; cook on low heat 15 minutes. Add juice of 1 lemon, dill and parsley. Stir with fork. Recover; cook 5 minutes or until all water is absorbed. Remove from heat; cool. To stuff grape leaves, spread 1 leaf, vein side up; fill with 1 teaspoon rice mixture. Fold and roll firmly in cigar shape, tucking in edges. Arrange rolled leaves in large saucepan. Mix together juice of 1 lemon, 3 tablespoons oil and 1 1/2 cups water. Pour over rolled vine leaves. Place tight fitting lid on saucepan. Cook 10 minutes on medium heat. Reduce heat; cook until water is absorbed, about 1 hour.

Makes about 60

See grape leaf rolling diagram at Yaprakis recipe. This dish is served at room temperature as a vegetable or an appetizer. Do not refrigerate if used on same day. Otherwise, refrigerate or freeze. When ready to serve add a little water; heat covered at 350° until just above room temperature. Cool to serve at room temperature.

PARVE *Sephardic Dinner 2007*

Avocado and Corn Salsa

1 ripe avocado

2-3 tablespoons fresh lime juice

1 ear sweet corn, cut off cob, not cooked

1 ripe red tomato, seeded, cut into 1/4-inch pieces

1 scallion, white and green parts, finely chopped

1-2 jalapeño or Serrano peppers, seeded, minced, for hotter salsa, leave in pepper seeds

1/4 cup chopped fresh cilantro

Coarse salt, kosher or sea, to taste

Freshly ground pepper to taste

Peel and cut avocado into 1/4-inch pieces. Cover with lime juice; gently toss to coat avocado. Set aside. Mix together corn, tomato, scallion, peppers and cilantro. Season with salt and pepper to taste. Add avocado; gently toss to mix all ingredients. Serve with corn chips.

Best in the summer when made with fresh farmer's market vegetables!

PARVE *Amy Labovitz*

Tomato Salsa

4 large tomatoes, peeled, seeded, chopped

1 large green bell pepper, seeded, cut into 1/2-inch pieces

1/2 cup chopped parsley

1/2-1 chopped jalapeño pepper, seeds and veins removed

1/2 teaspoon salt

1 tablespoon vegetable oil

Mix tomatoes, bell pepper, parsley, pepper, salt and oil. Cook until peppers are tender and juice has cooked down. Cover; refrigerate. Serve cold.

PARVE *Marie Berlin*

Joel's Garlic Salsa

1-2 tablespoons fresh cilantro, chopped

1-2 tablespoons garlic, minced

1 tablespoon lime juice, usually 1 lime

1 teaspoon salt

1 tablespoon sugar

1 jalapeño pepper, sliced

½ medium onion, sliced

1 pound Roma or plum tomatoes

Mix cilantro, garlic, lime, salt and sugar in blender until cilantro is finely chopped. Add jalapeño; blend until pepper is finely chopped. Add sliced onion; blend until coarsely chopped. Add tomatoes; blend until coarsely chopped. Cool in fridge 30 minutes.

Cilantro and peppers can vary in potency; add or cut back to taste. Chop onions and tomatoes to the size you like. The sugar is to counter the acidity of the tomatoes and lime. If your salsa tastes sweet, you've added too much! I choose Roma or plum tomatoes because their water content is low; experiment with other types, or try roasted tomatoes for a smoky taste.

PARVE   *Joel Kramer, son of Rabbi Scott and Rebbetzin Irene Kramer*

Hummus

1 (15 ounce) can garbanzo beans

1 large clove garlic, chopped

1 teaspoon salt

⅓ cup tahini

2 tablespoons water

Drain and rinse garbanzos. Put beans, garlic, salt and tahini in blender; blend until smooth. Refrigerate until ready to serve.

PARVE   *Amy Labovitz*

Black Bean Soup

1 onion, diced	1½ cups vegetable broth
1 teaspoon garlic powder	3 cups chunky salsa
1 tablespoon cumin	2 tablespoons lime juice
1 teaspoon crushed red pepper	Nonfat plain yogurt or sour cream, optional
2 tablespoons vegetable oil	
3 (16 ounce) cans black beans, undrained	

Cook onions, garlic, cumin and red pepper in oil over medium heat until onion is tender. Remove from heat. Puree 2 cans beans with liquid; add to sautéed onions. Add vegetable broth, remaining beans, salsa and lime juice. Heat mixture to boil, reduce heat to low. Simmer 30 minutes. Ladle soup into bowl, top with dollop of sour cream or yogurt, as desired. Serve with crackers.

PARVE OR DAIRY   *Dale B. Evans*

Borscht

1 (15-17 ounce) can beets with juice	1 onion, grated
2 cans water	Salt to taste
1 (15 ounce) can diced tomatoes, strained	Pepper to taste
	Lemon juice to taste
	Sugar to taste

Grate beets; use all juice. Add water, tomatoes, onion, salt, pepper, lemon juice and sugar. Boil 30 minutes. Cool to room temperature; refrigerate. When cold, add sour cream. Mix well.

Makes 4 bowls

DAIRY   *Joan Hanan*

Italian White Bean and Spinach Soup

1 tablespoon vegetable oil	1³/₄ cups chicken broth
1 medium onion, chopped	¹/₄ teaspoon coarsely ground black pepper
1 celery stalk, chopped	
1 garlic clove, finely chopped	¹/₈ teaspoon dried thyme
2 (15-19 ounce) cans white kidney beans, rinsed, drained	1 bunch (10-12 ounces) spinach, stems trimmed
2 cups water	1 tablespoon fresh lemon juice

In a 3-quart saucepan, heat oil over medium heat. Add onion and celery; cook until tender, 5-8 minutes. Stir in garlic; cook 30 seconds. Add beans, water, broth, pepper and thyme. Bring to boil. Reduce heat; simmer 15 minutes. Roll several spinach leaves together, like cigars; thinly slice. Repeat with remaining spinach; set aside. With slotted spoon, remove 2 cups beans from soup; reserve. Spoon ¹/₄ of soup into blender; puree until smooth. Pour into large bowl. Repeat with remaining soup. Return puree and reserved beans to saucepan. Heat to boiling over medium heat. Stir in spinach; cook just until wilted, about 1 minute. Remove from heat. Stir in lemon juice.

Makes about 7¹/₂ cups

MEAT   Leslie Capp

Crock Pot Chicken Taco Soup

3	cloves garlic	1	(8 ounce) can tomato sauce
2	celery stalks, chopped	1	cup canned diced tomatoes
1	large onion, chopped	½	cup chopped green chiles
1	medium green bell pepper, chopped	1	(12 ounce) can beer
2	(16 ounce) cans navy beans	1	teaspoon cumin
2	(15 ounce) cans black beans	1	tablespoon chili powder
2	(15 ounce) cans whole kernel corn, drained	2	teaspoons salt
		3	whole skinless, boneless chicken breasts

Place garlic, celery, onion, bell pepper, navy beans, black beans, corn, tomato sauce, tomatoes, chiles, beer, cumin and chili powder in crock pot; stir. Lay chicken breasts on top of mixture, pressing down until just covered by mixture. Set cooker on low heat; cover; cook 6 hours. Remove chicken breasts from soup. Cool; shred chicken. Stir chicken back into soup; continue cooking 1 hour. Serve topped with tortilla chips.

MEAT   *Bella Smith*

Chicken Vermicelli Soup

1 large onion, chopped

4 stems celery, chopped not too fine

3 carrots, trimmed, diced

2 (14.5 ounce) cans low sodium chicken broth

2-3 cups water

4 chicken bouillon cubes
Dash red pepper flakes

1 (14.5 ounce) can petite diced tomatoes

2 (16 ounce) cans crushed tomatoes

1 tablespoon vegetable oil

4 angel hair pasta nests or 4 ounces vermicelli

1 roasting chicken, cooked or one prepared rotisserie chicken, skinned, deboned
Juice of 1 lemon

Preheat oven to 350°. Place onion, celery, carrots, chicken broth, water, bouillon, pepper flakes, tomatoes and oil into a large pot or Dutch oven. Bring to boil; reduce heat; simmer until vegetables are tender. Toast vermicelli in baking pan in oven about 7 minutes or until pasta is lightly golden. Turn pasta once during browning. Cut chicken into bite size pieces. Break cooled vermicelli into pieces. Add chicken and vermicelli to vegetables; cook together until vermicelli is done. Add lemon juice. If liquid is too thick, add more chicken broth or water.

Taste for seasoning. Freezes well.

Serves 8 to 12

MEAT   Corinne F. Capilouto

Lentil Soup

2	large onions, chopped	1	(1 pound) package lentils
1	tablespoon vegetable oil	1	(15 ounce) can diced tomatoes
½	pound lamb or beef stew meat, with a soup bone or 2	5-6	chicken bouillon cubes
			Pepper to taste
1	(8 ounce) can tomato sauce		Dash red pepper flakes, optional
1	tomato sauce can water		Water

In large Dutch oven, sauté onion in oil, do not brown. Trim fat from meat; sauté with onions to brown lightly. Cover with tomato sauce and water. Simmer 30 minutes. While meat is simmering, pick through lentils; discard debris and discolored or pitted lentils. Rinse in strainer with cold water. Put lentils in 2-quart boiler; cover with water. Bring to boil; immediately empty into strainer; rinse with cold water. Add rinsed lentils, diced tomatoes, bouillon, pepper and red pepper flakes to meat. Cover with water, to about 1 inch above mixture. Bring to boil; reduce heat to simmer; cook until lentils are very tender, about 1 hour. Taste; adjust seasonings to taste. Serve with Sephardic rice.

MEAT   Corinne F. Capilouto

Pasta e Fagioli

2   tablespoons olive oil
1   medium onion, chopped
2   carrots, chopped
2   stalks celery, chopped
3   cloves garlic
8   cups chicken broth or vegetable broth
2   cups white beans, rinsed, drained

1   (14 ounce) can chopped tomatoes, undrained
    Salt to taste
    Pepper to taste
1   teaspoon dried thyme
½   head green cabbage, chopped
½   cup cooked pasta of your choice

Heat oil; add onion, carrots, celery and garlic. Sauté until vegetables soften, stirring often. Add chicken broth, beans, tomatoes and juice, salt, pepper and thyme. Bring to boil; add cabbage. Cover, reduce heat; simmer 30 minutes. Add pasta and serve.

You may substitute a handful of chopped green beans or zucchini cubes for cabbage.

Serves 6

MEAT OR PARVE   *Chris Ginsburg*

Onion Soup

4   large onions
¼   cup vegetable oil
46 ounces beef broth

⅓   cup dry red wine
¼   teaspoon salt or to taste

Thinly slice onions. Put oil in large pot; add onions. Sauté until limp but not brown. Add beef broth, wine and salt. Bring to boil. Lower heat; simmer 20 minutes. Place in serving bowls; top with toast points or croutons.

To make a dairy version, use butter and vegetable broth. Before boiling, add ¼ cup grated Parmesan cheese (dry, not fresh). After simmering, place soup in ovenproof serving bowl. Or, place in individual ovenproof soup bowls. Garnish with toast points or croutons, top with grated mozzarella cheese and broil until cheese melts.

Serves 6

MEAT OR DAIRY   *Diane Blondheim*

Baked Potato Soup

5	large potatoes, baked	6	cups milk
1/3	cup butter	1	teaspoon salt
1/2	large yellow onion, diced	1/2	teaspoon pepper
1	teaspoon minced garlic	1	cup sour cream
1/4	cup flour	1	cup grated Cheddar cheese

Scoop potato pulp into bowl; set aside. Melt butter in large pot. Add onion and garlic; sauté over medium heat. Add flour; mix well. Reduce heat to low. Add milk, salt and pepper. Mix in sour cream until smooth. Gradually add potatoes and Cheddar cheese. Stir occasionally. Cook over low heat until thickened. Serve hot.

Freezes well.

Serves 6 to 8

DAIRY   *Rebecca Robison Ternus*

Easy Potato Soup

1	medium onion, chopped	2	soup cans milk
1/2	cup margarine	10	medium potatoes, boiled, drained, cubed
1	(8 ounce) container French onion dip		Cheese, optional
2	(15 ounce) cans cream mushroom soup		Green onions, chopped, optional

Sauté onion in margarine in Dutch oven until tender. Add dip, soup and milk. Stir until soup is smooth. Add potatoes. Cook on medium heat until bubbly. Top with cheese or green onions, if desired.

Serves 6 to 8

DAIRY   *Kathie Cohen*

Potato and Leek Soup

2   tablespoons canola oil
1   medium onion, chopped
4   leeks, white parts only, chopped
4   medium large potatoes, sliced
      thin

4   cups clear chicken stock
    White pepper to taste
    Salt to taste

Heat oil in skillet. Add onion and leeks; sauté 3 minutes. Set aside. In large pot, cook potatoes in chicken stock until tender. Remove potatoes, reserving stock. Use ricer or blender to process potatoes; return to pot; add leeks, onions, pepper and salt. Simmer 10 minutes.

Freezes well.

Serves 4

MEAT   *Phyllis Kasover*

Chunky Gazpacho

2½ cups V-8 juice
1   cup peeled, seeded, finely
      chopped fresh tomatoes
¾   cup finely chopped celery
¾   cup finely chopped green bell
      pepper
¾   cup finely chopped green onion
3   tablespoons white wine vinegar

2   tablespoons extra-virgin olive oil
1   clove garlic, minced
1   tablespoon finely chopped fresh
      parsley
½   teaspoon kosher salt
½   teaspoon Worcestershire sauce
½   teaspoon pepper

Combine juice, tomatoes, celery, bell pepper, onion, vinegar, oil, garlic, parsley, salt, Worcestershire sauce and pepper in large glass or stainless steel bowl, do not use plastic. Stir; cover; refrigerate at least 6 hours before serving. Serve cold.

Serves 6

PARVE   *Jo Anne H. Rousso*

Gazpacho

½ cup oil

¼ cup vinegar

2 cups tomato juice

2 (16 ounce) cans tomatoes, undrained

1 medium-large cucumber, peeled, coarsely chopped

1 small-medium green pepper, coarsely chopped

1 stalk celery, coarsely chopped

Tabasco sauce to taste, optional

Croutons, optional

Combine oil, vinegar and tomato juice in large glass container. Set aside. Grate tomatoes, cucumber, green pepper and celery in blender. Add vegetables to juice. Add Tabasco sauce, if using. Stir to mix. Chill overnight. Garnish with croutons, if using.

Serves 6 to 8

PARVE   Linda Taffet

Rebbetzin Irene's Garden Vegetable Soup

⅔ cup sliced carrots

½ cup diced onion

2 cloves garlic, minced

3 cups fat-free broth, beef, chicken or vegetable

1½ cups diced green cabbage

½ cup cut green beans

1 tablespoon tomato paste

½ teaspoon dried basil

¼ teaspoon dried oregano

⅓ teaspoon salt

½ cup diced zucchini

Spray large saucepan with cooking spray; heat. Sauté carrots, onion and garlic over low heat until softened, about 5 minutes. Add broth, cabbage, beans, tomato paste, basil, oregano and salt; bring to a boil. Reduce heat; simmer, covered, about 15 minutes or until beans become tender. Stir in zucchini; heat 3-4 minutes. Serve hot.

Serves 4

MEAT OR PARVE   Irene E. Kramer

Grandma Brenner's Vegetable Soup

1	pound beef flanken (short ribs)	2	bay leaves
	Water	1	(16 ounce) can tomatoes
¼	cup pearl barley	1	green bell pepper, diced
1	medium yellow onion, coarsely chopped	½	cup fresh corn kernels
2	stalks celery, sliced	½	cup fresh lima beans
1	teaspoon Worcestershire sauce	1	medium potato, cubed
2-3	whole allspice	½	cup cut fresh green beans
2	whole peppercorns	½	cup sliced fresh okra
1	teaspoon kosher salt	1	cup sliced carrots

Place meat in large pot; cover with water. Bring to boil; reduce heat to simmer. Add barley, onion, celery, Worcestershire sauce, allspice, peppercorns, salt, bay leaves and tomatoes. Cover; simmer covered 1 hour or until meat begins to be fork tender. Add bell pepper, corn, lima beans, potato, green beans, okra and carrots; bring to boil. Add water if needed. Reduce heat to simmer; cook covered 1 hour. Taste; adjust seasonings to taste.

Freezes well. Skim fat from top before reheating.

MEAT   *Marian Shinbaum*

Vegetable and Barley Soup

4 tablespoons butter, margarine or oil, divided

2 onions, diced

½ cup pearl barley, rinsed well

1 pound fresh mushrooms, quartered, divided

10 cups vegetable or beef broth

2 large carrots, sliced

2 sticks celery, sliced

¼ cup chopped parsley

1 teaspoon dried dill weed

Salt to taste

Pepper to taste

1 tablespoon sour cream, optional garnish

Heat 2 tablespoons oil, butter or margarine in large soup pot. Sauté onions, barley and ½ of mushrooms. Add broth; bring to boil, stirring frequently. Reduce heat; simmer until barley is tender, about 30 minutes. While mixture is simmering, sauté remaining mushrooms with carrots and celery in remaining 2 tablespoons oil, butter, or margarine. Add to soup after simmering 30 minutes. Cook 20 minutes. Stir in chopped parsley and dill. Season with salt and pepper as needed. Serve hot.

If dairy, you may garnish each serving with 1 tablespoon sour cream.

Serves 6 to 8

MEAT, PARVE OR DAIRY   Dale B. Evans

Nan's Red Bean Chili

2   pounds lean ground turkey
1   large onion, chopped
½   green bell pepper, chopped
2   (8 ounce) cans tomato sauce
1   (15 ounce) can tomatoes with
       chiles
1   cup water
3½ tablespoons chili powder

1   teaspoon salt
1   clove fresh garlic
1   teaspoon oregano
2   tablespoons oil
2   tablespoons flour
2   (15 ounce) cans kidney beans,
       undrained

Brown ground turkey; add onion, bell pepper, tomato sauce, tomatoes, water, chili powder, salt, garlic and oregano. Cover; simmer 1 hour. In bowl, mix oil, flour and beans until smooth; add bean mixture to pot; cover; simmer 30 minutes, stirring occasionally.

Easy and enjoyable on a cold winter night.

MEAT   *Nan Lavin*

Nan's White Bean Chili

2   tablespoons vegetable oil
1   onion chopped
2   cloves garlic, minced
1   (14.5 ounce) can chicken broth
1   (10 ounce) can Rotel original diced
       tomatoes and green chiles
1   (7 ounce) can diced green chiles
1   (16 ounce) can Ortega Salsa
       Verde – medium

½   teaspoon dried oregano
½   teaspoon ground coriander seed
¼   teaspoon ground cumin
2   ears fresh corn
1   pound cooked chicken
1   (15 ounce) can white beans
1   pinch salt
1   pinch pepper

Heat oil in large Dutch oven; cook onion and garlic until soft. Stir in broth, tomatoes, chiles, salsa, oregano, coriander seed and cumin. Bring to boil; lower heat; simmer 10 minutes. Cut corn kernels off cob. Cut chicken into bite size pieces; add to soup. Add corn and beans. Simmer 5 minutes. Season with salt and pepper to taste.

MEAT   *Nan Lavin*

Vegetable Chili

3	(14.5 ounce) cans whole tomatoes	½	teaspoon dried oregano
2	(15 ounce) cans red kidney beans	½	teaspoon cumin
3	tablespoons olive oil	1	cup diced zucchini
1	small onion, chopped	1	cup diced yellow squash
2	cloves garlic, minced	2	cups diced carrots
3	tablespoons chili powder		Salt to taste
½	teaspoon dried basil		Pepper to taste

Drain and chop tomatoes, reserving juice; set aside. Drain 1 can kidney beans, set aside. In large pot, heat olive oil; sauté onion and garlic over medium heat until onion is soft, but not brown. Mix chili powder, basil, oregano and cumin; add all at once to onions. Cook 30 seconds, stirring constantly. Add zucchini, squash and carrots; cook 1 minute over low heat, stirring occasionally. Stir in tomatoes and juice, and all kidney beans. Bring to boil. Reduce heat; simmer, partially covered, 30-45 minutes, until thickened. Remove lid last 15 minutes if needed to encourage thickening. Season with salt and pepper.

Serves 4

PARVE *Nick G. Ashner*

White Chicken Chili

1	medium onion chopped	2	(15 ounce) cans Great Northern Beans
1	tablespoon olive oil		
1	(4 ounce) can chopped green chiles, drained	1	(14.5 ounce) can chicken broth
3	tablespoons all-purpose flour	1½	cups finely chopped cooked chicken breast
2	teaspoons ground cumin		

In large skillet cook onion in olive oil 4 minutes or until transparent. Add chiles, flour and cumin. Cook 2 minutes, stirring constantly. Add beans and chicken broth, bring to boil. Reduce heat; simmer 10 minutes or until thickened. Add chicken; cook until thoroughly heated.

Serves 4 to 6

MEAT *Carolyn Bern*

Broccoli Salad

2	cups coarsely chopped fresh broccoli	½	cup dry roasted peanuts
1	tablespoon minced onion	1	cup mayonnaise
½	cup golden raisins	½	cup sugar
		¼	cup red wine vinegar

Combine broccoli, onion, raisins and peanuts; mix well. 30 minutes before serving, mix mayonnaise, sugar and wine vinegar; blend well; pour over salad.

This can also be prepared the night before, but do not add the peanuts and dressing until 30 minutes before serving.

Serves 8 to 10

PARVE *Karen Herman*

Granny Lil Perlman's Marinated Slaw

1	large cabbage, shredded	½	cup oil
5	carrots, coarsely grated	1	cup cold water
1	large onion, chopped	3	teaspoons salt
2	green bell peppers, cut into thin strips	½	cup sugar
6	radishes, thinly sliced		Garlic powder or pepper to taste
⅔	cup vinegar		

Combine cabbage, carrots, onion, bell pepper and radishes. Set aside. Combine vinegar, oil, water, salt, sugar, garlic powder or pepper. Mix well; pour over vegetables. Chill overnight in refrigerator. Stir before serving.

PARVE *Carolyn Bern*

Crunchy Coleslaw

1 package chicken flavored ramen noodles	Flavor packet from noodles
½ cup sesame seeds	4 packages Equal or 6 tablespoons sugar
½ cup slivered almonds	1 tablespoon Accent
1 (10 ounce) package angel hair slaw	1 teaspoon pepper
2 green onions, sliced	½ cup vegetable oil
	½ cup rice vinegar

Preheat oven to 200°. Spray baking pan with cooking spray. Break ramen noodles into pieces and put on baking pan with sesame seeds and slivered almonds. Toast 45 minutes; cool. Combine slaw and onions. Mix together Ramen noodles flavor packet, Equal or sugar, Accent, pepper, oil and vinegar. Just before serving, add dressing to slaw; toss.

Serves 6

MEAT   *Wendy Finkelstein*

Cole Slaw

2 pounds shredded or thinly sliced purple cabbage	½ cup sugar
1 (10 ounce) bag matchstick carrots	½ cup vinegar
1 small onion, sliced very thin	¼ cup water
1 large green bell pepper, sliced very thin	½ cup vegetable oil
	4 teaspoons salt

Combine cabbage, carrots, onion and bell pepper. Mix together sugar, vinegar, water, oil and salt. Pour over cabbage; toss well. Marinate overnight.

PARVE   *Dana Handmacher*

Ruth Segall's Health Slaw

2½ pounds cabbage, about

3-4 carrots

2-3 cucumbers

1 green bell pepper

⅔ cup white vinegar

½ cup oil

¼ cup water

½ cup sugar

5 teaspoons salt, or to taste

⅛ teaspoon black pepper, or to taste

Shred cabbage; thinly slice carrots; dice, chop or thinly slice cucumbers; dice, chop or julienne bell pepper. If you use a food processor — shred. Carrots come out round, about the size of quarters. Combine prepared vegetables in large bowl. To prepare dressing, combine vinegar, oil and water. Stir in sugar, salt and pepper. Pour over vegetables; mix with hands. Let stand 15-20 minutes or marinate up to 24 hours. If you marinate 2 hours or more, volume shrinks in half. Drain excess liquid before serving. Re-season to taste.

Serves 12

We were young couples, just starting in synagogue life. Ruth shared many recipes and pearls of wisdom with us. This recipe in particular, is one enjoyed by lots of families for lots of years.

PARVE

Protégées of Ruth

Sweet and Tart Salad

3 cups shredded cabbage	4½ tablespoons cider vinegar, divided
½ cup dried cranberries, optional	1 teaspoon grated onion
½ cup sugar	1 cup vegetable oil
1 teaspoon dry mustard	1 tablespoon celery seed
½ teaspoon salt, optional	½ cup chopped apple

Toss together cabbage and cranberries, if using. Refrigerate. Mix sugar, mustard and salt, if using; add 2 tablespoons cider vinegar and onion. Gradually beat in vegetable oil until thick and light. Slowly beat in remaining cider vinegar. Stir in celery seed. Pour into screw-top jar; cover tightly; shake vigorously to blend well. Store covered in refrigerator. Makes about 1²/₃ cups. About 1 hour before serving, add apples to cabbage. Shake dressing well; pour over cabbage; toss lightly. Return to refrigerator until serving time. Toss before serving.

Serves 6

PARVE   Irene E. Kramer

Ruby's Chicken Salad

6 boneless, skinless chicken breasts, cooked, cooled and chopped	4 apples, peeled and chopped
	4 celery stalks, sliced
Garlic powder to taste	1 cup chopped toasted pecans
Salt to taste	¾ cup Craisins
Black pepper to taste	Mayonnaise

Season chicken with garlic powder, salt and pepper to taste. Add apples, celery, pecans and Craisins. Mix well. Add mayonnaise ¼ cup at a time. Stir thoroughly before adding more. The goal is to add just enough mayonnaise to hold the salad together but not make it too wet or soupy. Refrigerate at least 1 hour before serving.

Serves 6

MEAT   Dale B. Evans

Overnight Salad

³/₄ cup cider vinegar

½ cup salad oil

1 cup sugar

1 tablespoon water

1 teaspoon salt

1 teaspoon pepper

1 (15 ounce) can petite English peas, drained

1 (11 ounce) can white shoepeg corn, drained

1 (14.5 ounce) can French cut green beans, drained

1 cup chopped celery

1 cup chopped bell pepper

1 cup chopped green onions

1 (6 ounce) jar pimento, drained

Optional ingredients: bean sprouts, mushrooms, water chestnuts, whole baby corn.

Mix vinegar, oil, sugar, water, salt and pepper in saucepan. Bring to rolling boil. Remove from heat; cool completely. Place peas, corn, green beans, celery, bell pepper, onions, pimento and any optional vegetables you choose in a bowl; pour marinade over them. Cover tightly; refrigerate 24 hours, stirring occasionally.

This makes a lot, especially if you add some optional vegetables. You may substitute the English peas with artichoke hearts.

Serves 12 to 16

PARVE   *Margie Allen*

Ruth Segall's Marinated Cucumbers

¹/₃ cup vinegar

5 tablespoons water

5 tablespoons sugar

½ teaspoon salt

2 large cucumbers, peeled, sliced

1 medium Vidalia onion, sliced

Mix vinegar, water, sugar and salt. Pour over cucumbers and onions. Store in refrigerator. Keeps up to one week.

PARVE   *Betty Ehrlich & Elaine Kirkpatrick*

Beth Gewant Sherer's Easy Couscous Salad

1   (5.6 ounce) box couscous with pine nuts

1   cup cherry tomatoes, halved

1   cup peeled, cubed cucumber

1   (6 ounce) can artichoke hearts, drained, quartered

1   small onion, finely chopped, optional

Pine nuts for garnish

Salad dressing of your choice, a vinaigrette is best

Cook couscous according to package directions. Add tomatoes, cucumber, artichoke hearts and onion, if using. Add dressing; mix. Garnish with pine nuts.

Beth has also used the pearl/Israeli couscous. While the pearl couscous is yummy, it is definitely more work because you actually have to cook it.

Serves 4 to 6

PARVE   *Toby Gewant*

Israeli Salad

4   tablespoons olive oil

2   tablespoons white wine vinegar

Juice of 2 large or 3 small lemons

³/₄   cup finely chopped cauliflower

¹/₂   cup finely chopped onions

1   teaspoon salt

1   teaspoon freshly ground pepper

2   teaspoons finely chopped dried parsley

5   large tomatoes, seeded, diced

4   small salad cucumbers, peeled, diced

¹/₂   cup chopped green bell pepper

¹/₄   cup chopped yellow bell pepper

¹/₂   cup chopped fresh parsley

Combine oil, vinegar, lemon juice, cauliflower, onions, salt, pepper and dried parsley in a sealable jar. Shake to mix well. Refrigerate several hours, preferably overnight. Prepare tomatoes, cucumbers, bell peppers and fresh parsley. Pour dressing over vegetables; stir and refrigerate at least 1 hour. Stir and drain excess dressing before serving.

Serves 10

PARVE   *Jo Anne H. Rousso*

Beet Velvet Mold from Thelma Mendel

1   (3 ounce) package lemon Jell-O
1   cup boiling water
2   (4.5 ounce) cans strained baby
      food beets
1¼ cups sour cream, divided

1   tablespoon lemon juice
1   teaspoon grated onion
⅛   teaspoon Accent
      Dash of salt
      Dash of pepper

Dissolve Jell-O in boiling water; cool. Add beets, 1 cup sour cream, lemon juice, onion, Accent, salt and pepper; mix well. Pour into oiled mold. Chill until firm. When ready to serve, unmold; use ¼ cup sour cream for garnish.

   Serves 4

DAIRY   *Betty Ehrlich & Elaine Kirkpatrick*

Bing Cherry Mold

2   (3 ounce) packages black cherry
      Jell-O
2½ cups boiling hot water
½   cup cold Manischewitz Concord
      grape wine
2   (3 ounce) packages cream
      cheese, very cold

1   can pitted Bing cherries, drained,
      DO NOT USE JUICE
1   (6 ounce) can crushed
      pineapple, do not drain
½   cup chopped pecans

Dissolve Jell-O in hot water. Stir; add wine. Refrigerate 15 minutes or until Jell-O thickens. Grate cream cheese into Jell-O. Add cherries, pineapple and nuts. Refrigerate at least 2 hours or until congealed.

Cream cheese needs to be almost frozen so that it will be hard enough to grate.

   Serves 8

DAIRY   *Rita Rosenthal*

Blueberry Congealed Salad

2 cups water

1 (15 ounce) can blueberries, drained reserving juice

2 (8 ounce) cans crushed pineapple, drained, reserving juice

2 (3 ounce) packages black cherry Jell-O

1 (8 ounce) package cream cheese, room temperature

1 (8 ounce) container sour cream

½ cup sugar

1 cup chopped pecans, optional

Boil 2 cups water with 1 cup juice from fruit (½ cup blueberry, ½ cup pineapple). Discard remaining juice. Dissolve Jell-O in water and juice mixture; add fruit. Pour into greased 9x13 glass dish. Chill overnight. Blend cream cheese, sour cream and sugar. Stir in nuts; spread over top of Jell-O.

Can be used for salad or dessert.

Serves 15 to 24

DAIRY   *Kathie Cohen*

Frozen Cranberry Salad by Anna Lee Litvak

1 (14 ounce) can Eagle Brand milk

¼ cup lemon juice

1 (16 ounce) can whole cranberry sauce

1 (20 ounce) can crushed pineapple, drained

½ cup chopped pecans

1 (8 ounce) container Cool Whip, thawed

Combine Eagle Brand milk and lemon juice. Stir in cranberry sauce, pineapple and pecans. Fold in Cool Whip. Pour into 9x13 pan. Freeze until firm. When ready to serve, remove from freezer; cut into squares.

DAIRY   *Betty Ehrlich & Elaine Kirkpatrick*

Layered Vegetable Salad

1 head lettuce, torn in bite size pieces	1 (10 ounce) package frozen green peas, do not thaw
½ cup chopped onion	1½ cups mayonnaise
½ cup chopped celery	1 tablespoon sugar
1 (5 ounce) can sliced water chestnuts, drained	2 large tomatoes, diced
	4 hard-boiled eggs, sliced
	Grated American cheese

In large glass salad bowl, make an even layer of lettuce. Mix onion and celery; sprinkle over lettuce. Sprinkle water chestnuts, then unthawed peas. Spread mayonnaise evenly over top; sprinkle with sugar. Cover; refrigerate overnight. The next day, layer tomatoes, eggs and cheese over mayonnaise.

Serves 12

DAIRY   *Irene E. Kramer*

Aunt Della's Heartburn Salad

3 medium size white onions	1 (4.5 ounce) can mushroom slices, drained
1 green bell pepper	¾ cup oil
5 stalks celery	1 cup white vinegar
1 (3 ounce) jar pimiento strips, drained	1 teaspoon Accent
½ cup sweet pickle relish	½ teaspoon white pepper
	2 teaspoons salt

Coarsely chop onions, green pepper and celery; put in glass bowl. Add pimiento, pickle relish and mushroom slices. Mix together oil, vinegar, Accent, white pepper and salt. Pour over vegetables, mix well; marinate 2 days before serving.

Serves 8 to 12

PARVE   *Rita Rosenthal*

Mandarin Dried Cranberries Salad

2 tablespoons sliced almonds

1/4 cup olive oil

2 tablespoons sugar or dash Sweet & Low

2 tablespoons wine vinegar

1/2 teaspoon salt

1 tablespoon water

1 tablespoon fresh lemon juice

1/8 teaspoon pepper, or to taste

Bibb lettuce, romaine or bagged Italian lettuces, rinsed well

1/2 cup canned Mandarin oranges, well drained

2 tablespoons dried cranberries

Finely sliced Vidalia or red onion, about 3 slices per serving

Preheat toaster oven to 325°. Toast almonds about 8 minutes, or until lightly browned. Place olive oil, sugar, vinegar, salt, water, lemon juice and pepper in a jar; shake vigorously. Taste for sweetness; adjust as needed. Mix lettuce, oranges and cranberries. Place salad onto individual serving plates; drizzle with dressing; sprinkle with almonds. Separate onion slices into rings; place on top of salad.

Serves 2

PARVE *Corinne F. Capilouto*

Mandarin Orange Salad

1/4 cup slivered almonds

4 tablespoons sugar, divided

1 tablespoon butter

2 tablespoons vinegar

1/8 teaspoon almond extract

4 tablespoons salad oil

Salt to taste

Pepper to taste

1 cup diced celery

1 head lettuce

2 green onions, chopped

1 (8.25 ounce) can Mandarin oranges, chilled, drained

Brown almonds in 2 tablespoons sugar and butter in skillet over medium heat. Cool on foil; break into small pieces. Combine vinegar, 2 tablespoons sugar, almond extract, oil, salt and pepper to make dressing. Combine celery, lettuce and onions to make salad. Just before serving, add oranges and dressing. Gently toss. Top with almonds.

PARVE *Sue R. Jaffe*

Pasta Vegetable Salad

1 (6 ounce) package tri-color rotini pasta, about 3 cups
1 pound broccoli cut into florets
3 stalks celery, diced
1 bunch radishes, sliced
1 (8 ounce) can sliced water chestnuts, drained

1 (8 ounce) can sliced ripe olives, drained
1 (0.6 ounce) envelope zesty Italian salad dressing mix
2 tablespoons fresh chopped oregano
½ cup crumbled feta cheese

Prepare pasta according to package directions; cool. Combine with broccoli, celery, radishes, water chestnuts and olives. Prepare salad dressing according to package directions; stir in oregano. Pour over pasta and vegetables. Sprinkle with cheese. Cover; refrigerate overnight.

DAIRY   *Barbara Handmacher*

Lubel Potato Salad

6 large baking potatoes
1 medium bell pepper
1 medium onion
8 hard-boiled eggs, divided
2 stalks celery
1 (2 ounce) jar diced pimento, drained

1 tablespoon yellow mustard
5-6 tablespoons mayonnaise
1 tablespoon sweet pickle relish
   Salt to taste
   Pepper to taste

Wash and scrub potatoes. Boil covered 30 minutes or until tender. Drain; cool; cut into 1-inch cubes. Dice bell pepper, onion, 6 eggs and celery. Add to potatoes. Add pimento. Stir; toss to mix well. Blend together mustard, mayonnaise, pickle relish, salt and pepper. Mix into potato mixture. Thinly slice remaining two eggs for garnish.

Use about 1 hand-size potato per person. Make a day before serving, if possible. Just before serving, stir; add mayonnaise as needed.

Serves 8 to 12

PARVE   *Elaine Lubel Raymon*

Greek Quinoa Salad

1	cup quinoa		1	small red onion
4	cups water, divided		1/4	cup fresh parsley
2	lemons		1	tablespoon olive oil
1	vegetable bouillon cube		1	tablespoon balsamic vinegar
1	cucumber		1/4	cup feta cheese, more to taste
	Tomatoes, whatever variety you have on hand			Salt to taste
1/4	cup Kalamata olives, pitted, chopped			Pepper to taste

Soak quinoa 5 minutes in 2 cups water; rinse in colander. Zest lemons; set aside. Juice lemons; combine with 2 cups water, quinoa and bouillon cube; bring to boil. Cover; cook on low 15 minutes, until all liquid evaporates. Let quinoa sit 10 minutes; fluff with fork. Completely cool; you can put in fridge to speed up the process. Chop cucumber, tomatoes, olives, onion and parsley. Add lemon zest, olive oil and vinegar. Stir to mix. Add vegetables to quinoa; season with salt and pepper; add feta cheese on top.

You can add other vegetables to your liking. Quinoa is a complete protein, so it can be served as a well-balanced meal or as a side item.

PARVE   Jeanine Rousso

Greek Rice Salad

1	(7.2 ounce) package prepared rice pilaf mix	3	tablespoons red wine vinegar Juice of ½ large lemon
1½	cups chopped cucumber	1	clove garlic, minced
½	cup crumbled feta cheese	2	teaspoons dried oregano or dried mint
½	cup chopped parsley		
⅓	cup olive oil	1	large tomato, chopped

Prepare rice pilaf as package directs. Cool 10 minutes. Combine rice pilaf, cucumber, cheese and parsley in large bowl. Combine oil, vinegar, garlic and oregano. Pour over rice; gently toss. Cover; chill 4 hours or overnight. Stir in tomato just before serving.

DAIRY   *Jo Anne H. Rousso*

Naomi's Salad

1	large head Romaine lettuce	3	tablespoons red wine vinegar
1	large head escarole	2	teaspoons salt
6	scallions	½	teaspoon crumbled dried tarragon
4	avocados		
4	cups hearts of palm, drained Pimento strips, to taste	½	teaspoon pepper
5	tablespoons salad oil	1	clove garlic

Slice or cut up lettuce, escarole, scallions, avocados and hearts of palm any way you want. Add pimento strips. Combine oil, vinegar, salt, tarragon, pepper and garlic to make dressing. Pour dressing over salad just before serving. Gently toss to coat all lettuce.

> *I got this recipe from Naomi Gold. Naomi was a beloved Rebbetzin at Agudath Israel during the 1970's and 80's. I enjoyed this salad in Naomi's Sukkah and have served it many times.*

PARVE   *Barbara Handmacher*

Spinach Salad

2 Granny Smith apples, chopped, divided
½ cup golden raisins, divided
½ cup cashews, divided
1 (10 ounce) package fresh spinach

¼ cup sugar
¼ cup apple cider vinegar
¼ cup vegetable oil
¼ teaspoon garlic salt
¼ teaspoon celery salt

Reserve ¼ cup apple pieces, ⅛ cup raisins and ⅛ cup cashews for garnish; set aside. Remove stems; tear spinach into bowl. Combine remaining apples, raisins and cashews with spinach. Combine sugar, vinegar, oil, garlic salt and celery salt in a jar. Cover tightly; shake vigorously. Toss with spinach mixture. Garnish with reserved fruit and nuts.

Serves 6

PARVE　　　　　　　　　　　　　　　　　　　　　　　*Bella Smith*

Strawberry Spinach Salad

8 cups torn spinach
1 cup sliced mushrooms
3 kiwi fruit, peeled, sliced, divided
1 cup fresh strawberries, halved, divided

¾ cup coarsely chopped macadamia nuts or pecans, divided
2 tablespoons strawberry jam
2 tablespoons strawberry, raspberry or cider vinegar
½ cup vegetable oil

Combine spinach, mushrooms, half the kiwi, half the strawberries and half the nuts in large bowl; set aside. Place jam and vinegar in processor; process until combined. With machine running, slowly add oil. Pour dressing over spinach; toss gently. Divide among 8 salad plates; top with remaining kiwi, strawberries and nuts.

Serves 8

PARVE　　　　　　　　　　　　　　　　　　　　　　　*Irene E. Kramer*

Strawberry Salad

1	tablespoon butter	$1/2$	cup vegetable oil
$1/2$	cup pecan halves	$1/3$	cup sugar
1	tablespoon brown sugar	$1/2$	cup red wine vinegar
6	cups mixed greens	1	clove garlic, minced
1	cup shredded Monterey Jack or mozzarella cheese	$1/2$	teaspoon salt
		$1/4$	teaspoon paprika
$2^1/2$	cups sliced strawberries	$1/8$	teaspoon pepper

Melt butter in small skillet over low heat; add pecans and brown sugar. Cook; stirring constantly, 2-3 minutes or until caramelized. Cool on wax paper. In large bowl, mix greens, cheese and strawberries; set aside. Combine oil, sugar, vinegar, garlic, salt, paprika and pepper to make dressing. Mix well. Just before serving, pour over greens and gently toss.

Serves 4 to 6

DAIRY   *Bella Smith*

Fresh Fruit Salad with Citrus Dressing

2	cups fresh blueberries	2	peaches, peeled, sliced
2	cups fresh strawberries, sliced	$1/3$	cup orange juice
2	cups seedless grapes, any color	2	tablespoons lemon juice
3	kiwis, peeled, sliced	$1^1/2$	tablespoons honey
2	bananas, sliced	$1/4$	teaspoon ground ginger

Prepare fruit as close to serving time as possible, reserving bananas and peaches until last. Combine orange juice, lemon juice, honey and ginger. Just before serving, toss gently with fruit.

This healthy salad presents beautifully in a crystal or glass bowl.

PARVE   *Dale B. Evans*

Pickled Cabbage

2   large heads of cabbage
3-4   hot peppers per quart jar
4-5   cloves garlic per quart jar
1¼   cups good quality white vinegar
1   gallon hot water

½   cup salt
      Green bell peppers, carrot
      sticks, cauliflower florets,
      celery sticks, turnip roots cut
      into chunks, any combination,
      optional.

Sterilize 8-quart, or larger size jars in the dishwasher. Wash and cut cabbage into chunks. Put ½ of peppers and garlic cloves for each jar in the bottom. Fill with cabbage and other vegetables you choose. Add rest of peppers and garlic cloves on top. Mix vinegar with hot water and salt. Stir well to dissolve salt. Fill each jar with liquid. Reserve extra liquid; add to jars if needed after they sit overnight. Seal jars tightly. After 4 or 5 days, place in refrigerator.

PARVE   *Corinne F. Capilouto*

Bread and Butter Pickles

1   gallon thinly sliced cucumbers,
         small pickling variety
8   medium size onions, thinly sliced
2   green bell peppers, cut in half,
         thinly sliced
¼   cup kosher salt
1   cup water

3½   cups sugar
1   tablespoon mustard seed
½   teaspoon whole cloves
1   teaspoon celery seed
1½   teaspoons turmeric
2½   cups vinegar, more as needed

Combine cucumbers, onions and peppers in large roasting pan. Dissolve salt in water. Pour over vegetables. Add 3 cups ice cubes on top; let stand 3 hours; drain. Mix sugar, cloves, celery seed and vinegar in large pot; bring to boil. Add vegetables; add vinegar as needed to almost cover vegetables; heat to boil; remove from heat. Pack in sterilized quart jars immediately. Pack and seal each jar one at a time; don't set up an assembly line. Leave at room temperature for one week. Then store in refrigerator; they will remain crisp.

Makes 4 quarts

PARVE   *Clara Berns*

Sylvia Rubin's Pickles

2 (46 ounce) jars Mt. Olive whole Kosher Dill Pickles

6½ cups sugar

3½ teaspoons celery seed

2½ cups white vinegar

Several cloves of fresh garlic cut in half

Juice from 1 jar of pickles

Slice pickles and let sit on ice for 1 hour or longer. Combine sugar, celery seed, vinegar, garlic and pickle juice. Mix with sliced pickles. Place pickles and liquid in jars; store in refrigerator for 3-4 weeks before eating.

__PARVE__   *Dana Handmacher*

Papoo's Pickles

13 cups water

¾ cup plain salt

½ cup plain vinegar

Cucumbers, preferably 3 inches or less in length

½ teaspoon dill seeds or 4-6 inches fresh dill per jar

1 hot pepper per jar

1 clove garlic per jar

Bring water to boil; add salt. Mix until salt is completely dissolved; add vinegar. For each jar, fill until tight with cucumbers. Add dill, pepper and garlic. Completely cover with hot brine. Seal jars and let sit at room temperature for about 5-7 days. Then refrigerate.

Morris Rousso, my grandfather, made these pickles when my dad, Buddy, was a boy, and when my brother Eli and I were kids. Dad always wanted Papoo to make them hotter with more and more peppers and garlic. When I make them, I follow the recipe and they are delicious; just right.

__PARVE__   *Jeanine Rousso*

Dill Pickles

2/3	cup salt	2	cloves garlic per jar
3/4	cup white vinegar	1	sprig fresh dill or
15	cups water		1 teaspoon dill seeds per jar
1	hot pepper per jar	1½-2	pounds cucumbers
	Pinch of alum per jar		

Bring salt, vinegar and water to boil. Sterilize quart jars. Put hot pepper, alum, garlic and dill in each jar. Pack each jar with cucumbers. Fill each jar with hot brine. Seal jars. Store 1 week at room temperature, then refrigerate; they will keep better and stay crisp.

Makes 6 to 8 jars

PARVE *Clara Berns*

Red and Green Pepper Relish

12	red bell peppers	3	pints vinegar
12	green bell peppers	1¾	cups sugar
15	medium onions	3	tablespoons salt
1	bunch celery		

Wash peppers; remove cores and seeds. Peel onions. Wash celery; remove leaves. Finely chop in food processer. Cover with boiling water; let stand 5 minutes; drain well. Cover again with boiling water; let stand 10 minutes; drain well. Combine vegetables, vinegar, sugar and salt in large pan. Boil 15 minutes. Ladle boiling hot into 12 hot, sterilized half-pint jars. Seal at once as directed by jar manufacturer. Cool to room temperature before refrigerating.

PARVE *Jo Anne H. Rousso*

Specialties...

...passed down by generations!

Savory Pastries

Blintzes

Quiches

Kugels

These specialty recipes originate from the two distinctly different Jewish food cultures of our congregation — the Ashkenazi from Eastern Europe and the Sephardic from the Isle of Rhodes. These foods have been stimulating taste buds with their unique flavors for over 500 years. Amazing that we still have them and can preserve them within the pages of this cookbook.

Hints from the Experts

Many of these recipes were created when "from scratch" was the only option. Measurements have evolved from 1 glass of this and a handful of that to standard cups and tablespoons, but the art of preparing them remains much the same as when great-grandmothers brought them to America and Montgomery. Using the detailed directions and diagrams for some of these recipes will help you become an expert in no time!

Traditionally family members and friends get together to prepare these dishes. The work goes much faster and you can't beat the kitchen talk! Here are some helpful hints:

- Always read the entire recipe before you begin.
- If you're cooking alone, make half of the recipe.
- Prepare fillings before working the dough.
- Before you start, assemble equipment, utensils and supplies.
- Set up pans and areas for draining, resting dough and cooling.

With a little practice you will have them lining up for these delicacies just as they do at the synagogue and in our homes! Have fun, experiment, and share.

Boyos — Individual Savory Tarts

SPINACH FILLING

3   (10 ounce) boxes frozen chopped spinach

1-2 tablespoons flour

2½ cups grated Romano cheese, more to taste

¼   cup crumbled feta cheese, optional

2   teaspoons salt

Pepper to taste

Drain spinach in colander overnight; squeeze out excess liquid. Break spinach into small pieces; add salt and pepper. Add flour and cheeses; toss to coat each piece of spinach.

POTATO FILLING

3   pounds Idaho potatoes

1   cup cottage cheese

3   eggs, beaten

1   cup grated Romano cheese, more to taste

1   teaspoon salt

¼   cup feta cheese, crumbled

Peel and cut potatoes into cubes. Place in boiling water; simmer until fork tender; drain. Mash potatoes until smooth. Add cottage cheese, eggs, Romano cheese, salt and feta cheese; mix thoroughly. Add more cheese to taste.

DOUGH

¼   teaspoon yeast

½   teaspoon salt

2½ cups very warm water, divided

5¾ cups unsifted all-purpose flour, Pillsbury or Gold Medal, divided

Oil for pans

¼   cup grated Romano cheese, divided

Parmesan cheese for sprinkling

Preheat oven to 400°. Dissolve yeast and salt in ½ cup water; let stand 2 minutes. Sift 4 cups flour into large bowl. Using a wooden spoon, make a well in middle of flour; add yeast; gradually add 2 cups water. Stir until mixture becomes dough. Add small amounts of flour or water to achieve consistency of Play-Doh. With floured hands, knead dough in bowl until smooth and silky, not hard or tough. Cover; rest 20 minutes. Pour ½-inch oil into 2-inch deep pan; set aside. Sprinkle work surface lightly with flour. Place dough on surface;

BOYOS, CONTINUED ON NEXT PAGE

BOYOS, CONTINUED

knead until smooth. Divide into 6 equal pieces, knead one at a time until smooth. Flatten to shape of a hockey puck. Put balls in pan with oil. Turn over in oil, so both sides are oiled. Cover with wax paper; rest 20 minutes. Combine ³/₄ cup flour and 1 tablespoon grated cheese; set aside.

Take out 1 ball at a time, flatten slightly. Keep remaining balls covered until used. On flat oiled surface, roll dough from center out to double its original size. Pat dough with tiny bit of oil. Use oiled hands to stretch gradually until about 15 inches square or until paper-thin. Sprinkle with flour and cheese mixture and dab with fingertips dipped in oil. Repeat flour and oil coating between all layers, each time dough is folded. Bring dough's right ¹/₃ of rectangle to center, then left ¹/₃ to meet in middle. Do not overlap dough. Sprinkle with flour and cheese mixture; fold in half to make 4 layers. Cut dough into 4 equal squares; cut off any thick edges. Slightly roll out edge of each square. Stretch each portion into a 5-inch square. Pat with oil. In an oiled pan, make a layer of dough squares, cover with wax paper sprayed with cooking spray. Repeat with remaining squares.

Remove 1 square at a time from bottom of stack. Roll edges of square slightly. Place 2 tablespoons filling in center; fold each point toward center, each slightly overlapping the other, making sure filling spreads into corners. Place, crease side down, in well greased metal baking pan, ¹/₂-inch apart. Pierce each boyo with fork; sprinkle with Parmesan cheese. Bake 15-20 minutes or until golden brown. Bottom of boyos must be brown. Place on paper towel to drain.

Makes approximately 24

Dough may be refrigerated in oil up to 24 hours. To freeze, put each oiled dough ball in a fold-over sandwich bag; fold excess bag to encase dough ball. Lay flat in layers, no more than 2 layers in one container. Put foil between layers; tightly seal top with foil. Dough can be frozen up to 3 months.

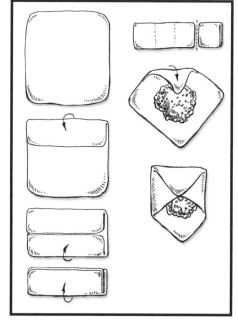

BOYOS, CONTINUED ON NEXT PAGE

BOYOS, CONTINUED

Sue Jaffe remembers: My sister, Joy Rousso, and I decided to make boyos for the first time many years ago, probably around 1975. We called Granny, Allegra Cohen, for instructions. She was great at doing, her food was the best of everyone's. However, she wasn't the best at teaching. She had us call Aunt Matilda Franco, who talked us through the process. I think it took about six calls when long distance cost real money. It was well worth every penny, they were delicious...but, not as good as Granny's or Aunt Matilda's!

DAIRY   *Traditional Sephardic Recipe*

Quick Boyos by Katherine Hanan

2	boxes puff pastry sheets	1	cup Parmesan cheese, or more to taste
3	large potatoes		
	Salt to taste	¼	cup cottage cheese or milk, more if needed
3	eggs, divided		

Thaw and open puff pastry sheets according to package directions. Preheat oven to 350°. Boil, drain and mash potatoes. Beat 2 eggs in medium bowl; add potatoes. Add Parmesan cheese. Add enough cottage cheese or milk so texture is soft, but firm. Beat remaining egg into a small bowl; set aside. Cut each sheet of puff pastry into thirds. Cut each strip into squares. Taking one square at a time, roll edges. Brush with beaten egg. Fill center with potato mix. Fold each point to meet in center without overlap. Dab points with water; press slightly. Place boyo, smooth side up, on lightly greased baking pan. Poke holes in top; brush with egg; sprinkle with Parmesan cheese. Bake 25 minutes.

Makes approximately 36

DAIRY   *Rochelle Koslin*

Burekas

POTATO FILLING

3	pounds russet potatoes
¼	cup butter
1	teaspoon salt
1½	cups grated Romano cheese, or more to taste

½	cup feta cheese, crumbled
½	cup cottage cheese, mashed, optional
3-4	eggs, beaten, divided

Peel and boil potatoes until tender. Add butter to hot potatoes; mash. Add salt, Romano, feta and cottage cheese, if using. Add 2 eggs. At this point, mixture may be refrigerated overnight, if desired. When ready to use filling, warm to room temperature; stir in remaining eggs until mixture is like stiff mashed potatoes. When dropped from a spoon, mixture will fall in peaks.

PARVE SPINACH FILLING —
See Boyo recipe on page 53 for traditional Dairy Spinach Filling

3	(10 ounce) boxes frozen chopped spinach
2	medium or 1 large onion, finely chopped
1	bunch green spring onions, finely chopped

2	tablespoons oil
1	tablespoon flour
1	teaspoon salt
1	teaspoon pepper

Thaw, rinse, drain and thoroughly squeeze dry spinach; set aside. Sauté onions and spring onions in oil. Add onions to spinach; add flour, salt and pepper. Toss and mix with hands; filling must be very dry and flaky.

DOUGH

8	cups White Lily all-purpose flour
3	cups water

1	cup vegetable oil
1	teaspoon salt

Preheat oven to 400°. Measure flour; sift; set aside. Bring water, oil and salt to a rolling boil. Remove from heat; use wooden spoon to quickly stir in flour as needed until dough is consistency of soft pie dough. It may not take all of flour.

BUREKAS, CONTINUED ON NEXT PAGE

BUREKAS, CONTINUED

While wearing rubber gloves to insulate your hands from hot dough, turn dough out onto a heat resistant board. Knead until smooth. Add flour as needed until dough is consistency of Play-Doh. Transfer dough to large bowl; cover with cloth dishtowel to prevent drying. Shape into walnut size balls. Roll each into a flat oval shape about 3x4 inches. Fill each oval with 1 rounded teaspoon filling. Fold in half; trim outer edge with rim of a small glass. Brush lightly with beaten egg; sprinkle with grated cheese. Place on well oiled baking sheet. Bake 20-30 minutes until golden brown. Cool on paper towels.

Makes 50 to 60

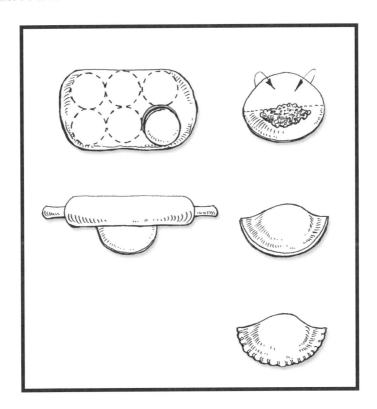

DAIRY   *Traditional Sephardic Recipe*

PARVE SPINACH FILLING   *Jeanette C. Rousso*

Pastelles — Individual Meat Pies

MEAT FILLING

2	onions	1	teaspoon salt
3	tablespoons oil	1/2	cup rice, rinsed
2	pounds ground beef	1/2	cup finely chopped parsley or celery
1/2	can tomatoes, strained through colander, reserve juice	2	hard-boiled eggs, optional
1/2	teaspoon pepper, optional		

Chop onions; sauté in oil until lightly browned. Add ground beef; sauté well, stirring constantly. Make a well in center; add tomatoes, pepper if using, salt and rice. Cover; simmer 25 minutes or until rice is well done. Add parsley or celery and chopped eggs, if using. Allow to cool.

DOUGH

1/2	cup vegetable oil	1	teaspoon salt
2 1/2	cups water	8	cups White Lily all-purpose flour

Bring water, oil and salt to boil; remove from stove; quickly stir in flour until consistency of soft pie dough. Knead until smooth, adding more flour if needed. Shape 3/4 of dough into 1-tablespoon size balls. Shape remaining dough into an equal number of 1-teaspoon size balls. Keep dough covered until ready to use. Preheat oven to 425°. Using thumb and forefinger, form large balls into hallow cups. Fill each cup to top with filling. Dip small ball into sesame seed. Flatten to be slightly bigger around than the cup opening. Press edges of cup and top together to seal, creating a rimmed edge. Using a small sharp knife, make short up and down cuts along edge of cap to form fringe. Pour small amount of oil into small bowl; with fingers, dab top of pastelles with oil. Place pastelles on generously oiled baking pan; bake until light brown on top, 30-40 minutes.

Instead of cutting a fringe edge, you may make a fluted edge. Place a finger against the inside edge of the pastry. Using the thumb and index finger of the other hand, press the pastry around the finger. Continue around the edge.

PASTELLES, CONTINUED ON NEXT PAGE

PASTELLES, CONTINUED

MEAT

Rojaldes – Phyllo Triangles

POTATO FILLING

2	pounds potatoes		1	cup cottage cheese or feta cheese
1	cup grated Romano or Parmesan cheese		1	teaspoon salt
			2-4	eggs

Peel, boil and mash potatoes. Mix in cheese, cottage cheese or feta and salt. Add eggs until mixture is consistency of stiff mashed potatoes. When dropped from a spoon, mixture will fall in stiff peaks.

SPINACH FILLING

3	pounds fresh spinach or 3 (10 ounce) packages frozen chopped spinach		$1\frac{1}{2}$	tablespoons all-purpose flour
$1\frac{1}{2}$	cups cottage cheese or 1 cup crumbled feta cheese		2	cups grated Romano cheese
			1	egg, beaten
			$\frac{3}{4}$	teaspoon salt

If using fresh spinach, chop fine in food processor. If using frozen, thaw, drain and squeeze out excess moisture, breaking into small pieces. Mix with cheese, flour, Romano cheese, egg and salt until all spinach is well-coated.

DOUGH

1	pound phyllo dough		1	egg, beaten with a drop of oil
1	cup vegetable oil			Sesame seed, grated Romano or Parmesan cheese

Remove phyllo dough from freezer; thaw in refrigerator overnight. Have filling ready before preparing phyllo for assembling. Keep dough covered with damp cloth until ready to use. Preheat oven to 350°. Place one sheet of phyllo on flat surface; dab lightly with oil. Place second sheet evenly over first. With a sharp knife, cut crosswise into 6 equal strips. Place 1 heaping teaspoon filling at lower corner of each strip. Fold filled corner into triangle. Continue folding

ROJALDES, CONTINUED ON NEXT PAGE

ROJALDES, CONTINUED

triangle shape to end of strip. Place rojaldes, side by side, in well-oiled baking pan. Brush tops with egg. Sprinkle with sesame seeds or grated Romano or Parmesan cheese. Bake 20 minutes or until lightly golden.

May be prepared ahead and frozen before baking. Layer between wax paper; store in tightly sealed container. Do not remove from freezer until ready to bake. Thaw to room temperature before baking.

Makes about 48

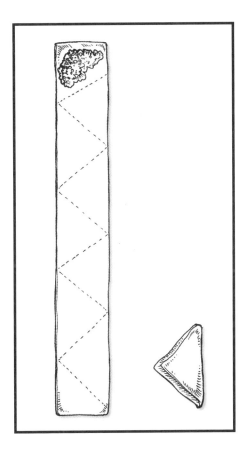

Aunt Betty's Blintz Soufflé

¼	cup margarine	2	tablespoons orange juice
6	frozen blintzes	2	tablespoons sugar
3	eggs	1	teaspoon vanilla
1	cup sour cream		

Preheat oven to 350°. Melt margarine in baking dish; coat both sides of blintzes. Place blintzes in baking dish. Combine eggs, sour cream, orange juice, sugar and vanilla; mix well. Pour mixture over blintzes. Bake 45 minutes.

Serves 6

DAIRY *Marsha Orange*

Aunt Goldie's Cheese Soufflé

8	slices challah bread, crust removed	2	cups milk
8	ounces grated sharp Cheddar cheese	8	eggs
		2	tablespoons butter

Preheat oven to 350°. Grease 9x13 baking pan with cooking spray. Starting with bread, layer with cheese, ending with bread. In blender, combine milk and eggs; pour over bread and cheese. Cover with aluminum foil, refrigerate overnight. Let stand at room temperature 1 hour before baking. Melt butter; pour over top. Bake 1 hour uncovered.

DAIRY *Linda Smith*

Blintz Casserole

Butter for sautéing and greasing pan

12 frozen cheese blintzes, thawed

4 eggs

2 cups sour cream, more if using for topping

1 teaspoon vanilla

³/₄ cup sugar

¹/₂ cup golden raisins, soaked in orange juice 30 minutes, drained

¹/₂ small orange, zested

Cinnamon to taste

Preheat oven to 350°. Melt butter; fry blintzes until golden. Place cooked blintzes in buttered 9x13 pan. Beat eggs with sour cream, vanilla and sugar; add raisins and orange zest. Pour mixture over blintzes. Sprinkle top with cinnamon. Bake 45 minutes or until custard is set and top is golden.

Serve with a dollop of sour cream, frozen strawberries in syrup or jam.

Serves 6

DAIRY *Margie Allen*

Orange Blintz Soufflé

4 eggs

¹/₂ cup sour cream

1 teaspoon vanilla

¹/₄ teaspoon salt

1 (6 ounce) can frozen orange juice concentrate

12 frozen blintzes

¹/₂ cup margarine

Preheat oven to 325°. Beat eggs well; add sour cream, vanilla, salt and orange juice concentrate. Mix well. Grease 9x13 pan. Place blintzes evenly in pan. Pour melted margarine then orange juice mixture over blintzes. Bake 1 hour 15 minutes.

DAIRY *Marsha Orange*

Hazel's Quajado

2 (10 ounce) packages frozen chopped spinach, defrosted, squeezed as dry as possible

8-10 large eggs

½ teaspoon salt, or to taste

½ teaspoon pepper, or to taste

¼ teaspoon garlic powder, or to taste

¼ teaspoon onion powder, or to taste

3-4 drops Tabasco, or to taste

2 cups cottage cheese

1 Secret Ingredient, can you believe it!!!! Kraft Macaroni and Cheese Dinner in a box

¼ cup grated sharp Cheddar cheese

1 cup grated mixed Parmesan-Romano cheese, more for garnish

Paprika to taste

Preheat oven to 325°. Put spinach in large mixing bowl. Put eggs salt, pepper, garlic powder, onion powder and Tabasco in blender. Blend well; add to spinach. Add cottage cheese. Now, for the secret ingredient! Cook macaroni according box directions. Drain; add ¾-1 cup to spinach. Mix cheese packet from dinner kit with Cheddar and Parmesan-Romano; add to spinach. Mix well. Butter two 8-inch square pans or one 2-quart rectangular Pyrex dish. Pour mixture evenly into pans. Sprinkle top with Parmesan-Romano and paprika for color. Bake 45 minutes or until nicely browned on top. Let cool; cut into squares to serve.

Every since I was a little girl, there was a standing joke about my Mom's quajados. Her Sephardic friends always joked that "Ashkenazi Hazel" made a quajado as good or better than the crème de la crème of the Sephardic cooks, but with a deliciously different twist. (If you don't believe me, just ask Jeanette Rousso, Corinne Capilouto, or Joan Hanan) When Mamma passed away I found her recipe. I couldn't believe her "Secret Ingredient". Now it's time to disclose "Hazel's Quajado" to the rest of the world. I am delighted to share the "Big Reveal"! I hope you enjoy it as much as I did when Mamma used to make it.

No Mac Quajado Cups

1 (10 ounce) package frozen chopped spinach
½ cup onion, chopped
1½ cups liquid egg substitute
1 cup cottage cheese
1 cup Romano cheese
8 drops hot sauce

Preheat oven to 350°. Line 12-cup muffin pan with foil baking cups. Spray cups with cooking spray. Thaw spinach; drain and squeeze dry. Add onion, egg substitute, cottage cheese, Romano cheese and hot sauce to spinach. Mix well. Divide evenly among cups. Bake 25-30 minutes or until knife inserted in middle comes out clean and tops are slightly browned.

Serves 12

DAIRY   Jo Anne H. Rousso

Zucchini Squares

4 eggs
3 cups zucchini, sliced thin
1 cup Bisquick
½ cup chopped onion
¼ teaspoon oregano
¼ teaspoon black pepper
½ teaspoon salt
   Garlic powder to taste
2 tablespoons fresh parsley
½ cup Parmesan cheese
½ cup oil

Preheat oven to 350°. Beat eggs in large bowl. Add zucchini, Bisquick, onion, oregano, pepper, salt, garlic powder, parsley, cheese and oil. Mix well. Spray 9x13 Pyrex pan with cooking spray. Pour mixture into pan. Bake 30-35 minutes, until golden brown. Cut in small squares for appetizer or larger squares for brunch or vegetable side dish.

DAIRY   Esther Miller

Quajado

2	(10 ounce) packages frozen chopped spinach	7-9	large eggs, beaten, divided
2	cups shredded Romano cheese, divided	1/2	cup crumbled feta cheese
1/2	teaspoon salt, divided	1/2	cup cottage cheese
1	cup uncooked elbow macaroni	1/8	teaspoon black pepper
		3	tablespoons vegetable oil
		1/4	cup grated Parmesan cheese

1 to 24 hours before baking, defrost, wash, drain and squeeze spinach dry into a medium bowl. Add 1/2 cup Romano cheese and 1/4 teaspoon salt. Mix well. Use immediately or cover and refrigerate for up to 24 hours. When ready to bake, preheat oven to 400°. In a medium size saucepan, bring 3 cups water to a boil. Add 1/4 teaspoon salt. Add macaroni; cook until barely tender. Drain into colander; rinse immediately with cold water. Retrieve spinach and cheese mixture from refrigerator. Add remaining Romano cheese, 6 beaten eggs, feta cheese, cottage cheese and pepper. Mix until well incorporated. Mixture should look moist, with some of the eggs visible. If too dry, add beaten eggs, one at a time until moist enough. Spray 2-quart glass baking pan with cooking spray. Add vegetable oil. Heat pan for 5 minutes. Drop about 1 teaspoon hot oil from pan into spinach mixture; mix thoroughly. Pour spinach mixture into pan. Spread 1-2 beaten eggs over top; drizzle liberally with Parmesan. Bake 40-45 minutes or until browned and center is completely set. Use crumpled paper towels to wipe away any excess oil from edges of pan. Loosely cover pan with wax paper; cool on a wire rack 10 minutes before cutting into squares for serving.

To freeze, cool completely in pan; tightly cover and freeze up to 3 months.

Serves 12 to 16

QUAJADO, CONTINUED ON NEXT PAGE

QUAJADO, CONTINUED

Quajado is a very popular dish in Sephardic homes. Everyone's is a little bit different and everyone thinks her mother's was the best. The amounts for the cheeses, eggs and macaroni change from family to family. It is a dish I am asked to make for the Hanukkah Hoopla, parties, holidays, shiva meals, and family gatherings. A take-home quajado for my grandchildren, nieces and nephews is part of almost every family celebration.

DAIRY   *Jeanette C. Rousso*

Artichoke Frittata

2	tablespoons olive oil	1/2	cup shredded Swiss cheese
1/2	cup chopped onion	1/2	cup shredded Cheddar cheese
1	clove mashed garlic	2	tablespoons minced parsley
1	(14 ounce) can artichoke hearts	1/2	teaspoon salt
4	eggs	1/8	teaspoon pepper
1/4	cup breadcrumbs	1/4	teaspoon oregano

Preheat oven to 350°. Sauté onion and garlic in oil until limp. Remove from heat. Drain; chop artichoke hearts; add to onions and garlic. Beat eggs well; add to mixture. Add breadcrumbs, Swiss and Cheddar, parsley, salt, pepper and oregano; mix well. Spray 7x11 pan with cooking spray. Pour mixture into pan; bake 30 minutes. Cool 10 minutes; cut into squares.

Serves 10

DAIRY   *Esther Miller*

Spinach Quiche

3   frozen pie crusts, thawed
3   cups shredded Jarlsberg cheese
3   (10 ounce) packages frozen chopped spinach, thawed, well drained
2   cups heavy whipping cream, not whipped
2   cups milk
6   eggs
1   medium onion, diced
$1/2$ cup flour
$1^1/2$ teaspoons salt
$1/2$ teaspoon pepper

Preheat oven to 400°. Sprinkle cheese evenly over pie crusts; evenly distribute spinach over cheese. Combine cream, milk, eggs, onion, flour and salt and pepper. Mix well; pour over pies. Bake 30 minutes or until top is brown and center is set.

May substitute $1/2$ cup Swiss or Munster, instead of all Jarlsberg. Freezes well. Great for lunch or light supper.

DAIRY   *Marion Varon*

Zucchini Quiche Miniatures

3   cups zucchini, chopped fine
1   small onion, chopped fine
4   eggs
1   cup canola oil
$1/2$ cup shredded Swiss or mozzarella cheese
$1/2$ teaspoon ground oregano
1   teaspoon parsley flakes
$1/4$ teaspoon salt
$1/2$ teaspoon pepper

Preheat oven to 350°. Spray 2 miniature muffin pans with cooking spray. Mix zucchini, onion, eggs, oil, cheese, oregano, parsley, salt and pepper. Divide batter evenly into pans, almost to top. Bake 40-45 minutes until brown, do not overcook. Cool in pans on wire rack. Quiche should tumble from pans when cool.

Makes 48

DAIRY   *Mickey Feldman*

Apricot Kugel

1   (16 ounce) package extra wide egg noodles, boiled, well rinsed and drained
1½ cups unsalted butter, melted
5   eggs, beaten
3   (8 ounce) containers sour cream
1½ cups sugar
1   teaspoon vanilla extract

2   (20 ounce) cans crushed pineapple, drained
1   package dried apricot halves, diced into small pieces
1   package dried apple slices
    Ground cinnamon, to taste
    Sugar or sugar substitute, to taste

Preheat oven to 375°. Place noodles in large mixing bowl. Add butter. Add eggs, sour cream, sugar, vanilla extract, pineapple and apricots. Mix well by hand. Spray 9x13 Pyrex baking dish with cooking spray. Line bottom of dish with apple slices. Fill to top with noodle mixture. Mix cinnamon with sugar; sprinkle on top. Bake 45 minutes to 1 hour.

You may have extra noodles and fruit mixture; bake in a small pan for yourself, for a friend or neighbor.

Serves 12 to 16

DAIRY   *Rita Rosenthal*

Nancy Shinbaum's Award Winning Kugel

1   (12-16 ounce) package egg noodles, cooked
4   tablespoons butter, melted
4   eggs
½   cup sugar

1   tablespoon almond extract
½   cup slivered almonds
1   cup maraschino cherries, cut up with some juice added

Preheat oven to 350°. Mix butter, eggs, sugar, almond extract, almonds, cherries and juice. Add noodles; mix well. Pour in a greased 9x13 baking dish. Cover. Bake 45 minutes.

Serves 8

DAIRY   *Nancy Shinbaum*

Noodle Pudding

8 ounces medium broad noodles	3/4 cup + 6 tablespoons margarine, melted, divided
3 ounces cream cheese	
3/4 cup milk, divided	1 cup crushed corn flakes
3 eggs	1 teaspoon cinnamon
3/4 cup sugar, divided	1/4 cup sugar
3/4 cup apricot nectar	6 tablespoons margarine, melted

Preheat oven to 400°. Spray 8-inch square pan with cooking spray. Cook noodles according to package directions, slightly overdone. Mix cream cheese with 1/4 cup milk until creamy. Set aside. Beat eggs and sugar until creamy. Add 1/2 cup milk and apricot nectar. Blend well; add melted margarine and cream cheese mixture. Pour noodles into prepared pan. Evenly spread egg mixture over noodles. Combine corn flakes, cinnamon, 1/4 cup sugar and 6 tablespoons margarine; sprinkle over noodles. Bake 45 minutes.

Serves 6 to 8

DAIRY   *Marsha Orange*

Oven Noodle Pudding by Ruth Segall

1 (8-10 ounce) package fine noodles	1 (8 ounce) can crushed pineapple
3 eggs	1 cup white raisins
3/4 cup sugar	2 tablespoons corn flake crumbs
1 cup sour cream	2 tablespoons sugar
1 (16 ounce) container cottage cheese	Butter to taste

Preheat oven to 350°. Boil noodles per package instructions. Drain. Beat eggs and sugar; add sour cream. Drain pineapple; save juice. Add pineapple, cottage cheese, noodles and raisins to sour cream. Stir to mix. Pour into well buttered 9x13 pan. Drizzle reserved pineapple juice on top. Sprinkle corn flakes and sugar; dot with butter. Bake 45 minutes.

DAIRY   *Hazel & Janice Segall*

Entrées...

...traditional and new main courses!

Meat

Poultry

Fish

Vegetarian

Jewish women through the centuries have used their ingenuity to get the most out of local meats, such as brisket and ground beef. And they certainly became masters at creating new ways to serve chicken for Shabbat. Other center plate recipes include contemporary pastas and vegetarian selections. Both are healthy choices that you will enjoy!

Lisa's Corn Beef

2-3 tablespoons vegetable oil
2-3 pounds beef brisket
2-3 tablespoons pickling spice

½ teaspoon granulated garlic
Water

Lisa's directions: preheat oven to 350°. Heat oil in metal baking pan. In an iron skillet, sear brisket on both sides, 2-3 minutes per side. Add pickling spice and garlic. Add 1½-2 cups water. Seal with aluminum foil. Bake 3½-4 hours. Remove brisket. Carve against grain. Mom's way: place brisket in slow cooker. Add pickling spice, garlic and 4 cups water. Cook 7-8 hours on low. Remove brisket; carve against grain. My way: heat oil in pressure cooker. Sear brisket on both sides, 2-3 minutes per side. Add pickling spice and garlic. Add 1½-2 cups water. Lock lid; bring to high pressure. Lower heat; maintain pressure; cook 1 hour. Natural release. Remove brisket. Carve against grain.

MEAT   Nick G. Ashner

Barbeque Short Ribs of Beef

2 tablespoons oil
3 pounds beef short ribs
1 medium onion, chopped fine
½ cup celery, chopped fine
¼ cup vinegar

1 cup ketchup
2 tablespoons sugar
2 teaspoons salt
3 tablespoons Worcestershire sauce
1 teaspoon prepared mustard

Preheat oven to 350°. Heat oil in Dutch oven; brown ribs on all sides. Remove ribs; sauté onions in same pan until soft. Place ribs back in pan; add celery, vinegar, ketchup, sugar, salt, Worcestershire and mustard. Cover; bake 1½-3 hours, until meat falls off bones. Skim off excess fat and let cool. Remove bones, leaving just meat in sauce. Heat in microwave or on stovetop, covered, stirring often to heat evenly.

Freezes well. Thaw in refrigerator 12 hours.

Serves 4

MEAT   Nick Ashner

Keftes De Carne – Meat Patties

1 pound ground beef	1 cup tomato sauce
2 eggs, divided	1 cup water
1 slice bread, soaked in water	Pinch sugar
1 tablespoon parsley	1/2 teaspoon salt
1 1/2 teaspoons salt, divided	Juice of 1 lemon
Pepper to taste	1 onion or 1 clove garlic, minced, optional
1/2 cup flour	
Oil for frying	

Preheat oven to 350°. Mix together meat, 1 beaten egg, bread, parsley, 1 teaspoon salt and pepper. Shape into 12 patties. Coat each patty with flour, dip in 1 beaten egg; fry in oil until both sides are golden brown. Combine tomato sauce, water, sugar, 1/2 teaspoon salt, lemon juice and onion or garlic, if using, in small bowl. Place patties, overlapping, in baking dish, pour sauce over patties; cover; bake 30 minutes. Uncover; bake 10 minutes.

For Passover, use 1/4 cup matzah meal instead of bread to make keftes and coat with matzah meal instead of flour.

Makes 12

MEAT   *Traditional Sephardic Recipe*

Yaprakis – Grape Leaves Stuffed with Meat

1 cup dried great Northern beans, or 2 (14-16 ounce) cans, rinsed, drained

1 (8 ounce) jar grape leaves, rinsed, drained

1 pound lean ground beef

¼ cup rice, rinsed, drained

1 teaspoon salt

Pepper to taste

1 tablespoon + 2 teaspoons oil

Juice of 1½ lemons, divided

¼ cup chopped parsley or celery leaves

¼ cup + 2 tablespoons tomato sauce

2 cups water

If using dried beans, cover in water; boil 30 minutes. Rinse and pat dry grape leaves; remove stems by cutting a slit in the leaf on each side of stem; set aside. Mix ground beef, rice, salt, pepper, 1 tablespoon oil, juice of ½ lemon, parsley or celery and 2 tablespoons tomato sauce; set aside. Mix 2 teaspoons oil, ¼ cup tomato sauce, water and juice of 1 lemon to make sauce; set aside. Reserve 6-8 leaves. To roll remaining leaves, lay a leaf flat, vein side up, with point of leaf at the top. Place about 1 teaspoon filling on leaf. Turn up bottom edges of leaf, tuck in side edges. Roll to tip in cigar shape, keeping edges tucked in. Rinse and drain beans. Place beans and rolls in saucepan in layers. Start and end with beans; pack rolls tightly. Pour sauce over all. Cover with reserved grape

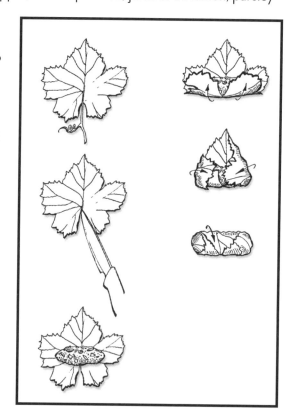

YAPRAKIS, CONTINUED ON NEXT PAGE

YAPRAKIS, CONTINUED

leaves. Place small, heat-resistant plate on top, pressing down. Cover with saucepan lid; cook slowly 45 minutes. Add juice of 1 lemon, re-cover; cook 15 minutes or until tender.

> Sue Jaffe remembers: My great Uncle Victor Cohen learned to cook all his favorite foods after Aunt Matilda passed away. The week after my father, Morris Rousso, passed away, he came to my mother's house with a large pan of yaprakis he made. They were as wonderful as any made by the women. He said his secret was adding a little water to the meat mixture. He learned to make many of the Sephardic foods so he could enjoy them as he always did when Aunt Matilda was the cook in their home.

MEAT   *Sephardic Dinner 2007*

Pot Roast for the Crock Pot

3-4	pound beef chuck roast		3	tablespoons flour
2	large potatoes, chopped		1	package brown gravy mix
3/4	pound baby carrots		3/4	cup hot water
2	onions, chopped		3/4	cup bottled Italian dressing
3	stalks celery, chopped			

Spray crock pot with cooking spray. Place roast into crock pot. Cover with potatoes, carrots, onions and celery. Sprinkle with flour. Combine gravy mix, water and Italian dressing. Pour over roast. Cover; cook on low 8-10 hours or on high 5-6 hours.

MEAT   *Sandi Stern*

Grandma Herman's Stuffed Cabbage

1	large head cabbage	1	(15 ounce) can tomato sauce
1	pound ground beef	1	(15 ounce) can water
½	cup uncooked rice	1	(10.75 ounce) can tomato soup
½	teaspoon kosher salt	1	tablespoon lemon juice
	Dash pepper	½	cup brown sugar
	Toothpicks	¼	cup granulated sugar
1	large onion, thickly sliced	1	(16 ounce) can sauerkraut

Soften cabbage leaves in boiling water; cool. Remove leaves from stem. In bowl, combine beef, rice, salt and pepper. Place about 1 tablespoon of mixture on each leaf. Roll up, starting with stem end. Tuck ends in. Secure with a toothpick; set aside. Cut up remaining cabbage; place in a large pot; layer onion slices next; place cabbage rolls on top. Mix tomato sauce, water, tomato soup, lemon juice, sugars and sauerkraut. Pour over cabbage rolls. Cover; cook slowly 2-2½ hours.

Can make ahead. Can freeze.

Serves 6

Passed on lovingly from Grandma Anne Gardner Herman to Judy Herman Shujman, Anne's only granddaughter.

MEAT   Judy Herman Shujman

Rolled Cabbage

2   small heads cabbage, cored
1   (28 ounce) jar sauerkraut
1   (46 ounce) jar tomato juice
³/₄ cup dark brown sugar
³/₄ cup white granulated sugar
3   pounds ground beef

Salt to taste
Pepper to taste
Garlic powder to taste
3   slices white bread, or 3 pieces matzah if Passover

Preheat oven to 350°. Boil cabbage 30 minutes; drain; separate leaves; cool. In large pot, mix sauerkraut, tomato juice and sugars; heat 5 minutes to dissolve sugar; set aside. In large mixing bowl, lightly mix meat, salt, pepper and garlic powder. Soak bread or matzah in ice water; squeeze out water; shred into meat mixture; lightly mix. Lay a cabbage leaf on flat surface. Place about 2 tablespoons meat mixture at stem end of leaf. Fold leaf over meat, tucking in sides and end, to make a neat roll. Place rolls, touching each other, into large roasting pan. Layer until pan is filled. Pour sauerkraut mixture over rolls; spread to cover all. Bake 3 hours uncovered.

Makes 24 to 26 rolls

MEAT   Diane K. Blondheim

Hazel Aronov's Stuffed Cabbage

1   (15 ounce) can tomatoes, drained, reserve juice
1   slice rye bread
1½ pounds ground chuck
½   cup instant rice, optional
1   egg
1   small onion, grated

Salt to taste
Pepper to taste
1   large cabbage, cored
    Juice of 1 lemon
3   tablespoons brown sugar or brown sugar sweetener
1   cup ketchup

Soak bread in tomato juice. Put meat in medium bowl; add rice if using. Mix; set aside. Combine tomatoes, bread, egg, onion, salt and pepper in blender. Blend until smooth; add to meat. Mix until well blended. Boil cabbage until leaves are pliable; separate leaves. Roll meat mixture in leaves; secure with toothpick; put rolls in heavy skillet. Mix together lemon juice, brown sugar and ketchup. Pour over cabbage. Cover; simmer 1 hour. If desired, uncover; put in hot oven to brown.

MEAT   Rhonda Blitz

Ruth Segall's Stuffed Cabbage

1	head cabbage	½	cup golden raisins, optional
1	large onion, chopped	1	apple, grated, optional
	Oil for sautéing	6	gingersnaps, crumbled, optional
2	(8 ounce) cans tomato sauce	2	pounds ground beef
1	(28 ounce) can Italian tomatoes or tomato purée	⅓	cup uncooked rice
¼	cup ketchup	½	cup water
½	cup brown sugar	1	teaspoon salt
¼	cup lemon juice	¼	teaspoon pepper

Boil cabbage 10 minutes. Take out core; separate leaves; scrape or cut off tough stems. Dice innermost leaves. Set aside whole leaves. Sauté onion in a little oil in large Dutch oven. Add diced cabbage. Add tomato sauce, tomatoes, ketchup, brown sugar and lemon juice. Add raisins, apple and/or gingersnaps, if using. Bring to boil, stirring often. Remove from heat. Taste for seasoning and sweet and sour flavor. To prepare filling, combine ground beef, rice, water, salt and pepper. Put about 2 tablespoons filling on each cabbage leaf; roll securely, tucking in sides. Put rolls into sauce. Cover. Cook on low heat 1½ hours, or bake in 300° oven 2 hours, covered.

Making a day before serving and reheating uncovered in 350° oven improves the flavor. The sauce is so good; you will probably want to make double. Freezes well; try individual plastic baggies.

This was one of my mother's favorite dinners to pull from the freezer, reheat in the microwave and serve to my father.

Hazel Segall

Calavasa, Sevollas, or Tomates Reinados - Stuffed Squash, Onions or Tomatoes

1	slice bread, soaked, squeezed dry	10-12	medium yellow squash or 12 medium onions or 6-7 medium tomatoes
1	pound ground beef	½	cup all-purpose flour
2	eggs, beaten, divided	½	cup tomato sauce
1	tablespoon parsley or celery leaves, chopped	½	cup water
1½	teaspoons salt, divided	½	teaspoon sugar
	Pepper to taste		

Preheat oven to 300°. Spray 8x8 baking dish; set aside. Prepare vegetable you choose: Peel squash; cut off stems; then halve lengthwise. Scoop out pulp; place pulp and stems in baking dish. Cut onions in halves lengthwise; separate outer layers in double thicknesses. Chop inner portions; place in baking dish. Cut tomatoes in halves; scoop out pulp; place in baking dish. Mix bread, beef, 1 egg, parsley or celery, salt and pepper. Stuff vegetable with meat mixture. Dip meat side into flour, then beaten egg. Brown meat side in small amount of oil; turn; cook 30 seconds; place in baking dish, meat side up. Combine tomato sauce, water, sugar and ½ teaspoon salt; pour over top. Bake, covered 1 hour. Uncover; bake 10 minutes.

You can also use bell peppers. You may cook any combination of these vegetables in the same pan. For Passover, substitute matzah meal for flour.

Serves 10 to 12

I serve a stuffed vegetable along with a meat entrée on many Friday nights for my family. Add Sephardic rice, fasulia or bamia and a salad – you've got it made! And, there is always at least one stuffed vegetable on the menu for almost every holiday.

Jeanette C. Rousso

Toby's Barbecued Brisket

5   pounds first-cut brisket
     Garlic powder
     Onion powder
     Celery salt

2-3 small bottles liquid smoke
1/2-1 small bottle apricot or tomato
     jam
1   (28 ounce) bottle sweet
     barbecue sauce

Preheat oven to 250°. Sear meat on barbecue grill; cook off as much fat as possible. Place large piece of heavy-duty foil in broiler pan. Place meat on foil. Liberally sprinkle with garlic powder, onion powder and celery salt; rub into meat. Pour liquid smoke over meat. Cover meat with another large piece of foil; roll and crimp all sides of both pieces of foil. Roast 3 hours. Cool in pan; refrigerate overnight, makes slicing much easier. To slice, cut off more fat if necessary; slice across grain. Soften jam in microwave; combine with barbecue sauce. Pour a little sauce in a 9x13 glass baking dish. Place brisket on sauce. Pour remaining sauce over brisket, making sure sauce seeps in between slices. Cover; roast 1 hour.

If freezing for future use, after pouring on sauce, cover well and freeze. Defrost in refrigerator the day before serving. On serving day, bring to room temperature; roast 1 hour. I think this second roasting makes the meat very tender. If you can find tomato jam, try it; it is yummy!

Serves 8 to 10

MEAT   Toby Gewant

Beer Brisket

5	pounds brisket	2	teaspoons salt
2	onions, sliced	1/4	teaspoon pepper
4	celery stalks, whole	1/4	cup water
1	(12 ounce) bottle chili sauce	1	(12 ounce) can beer

Preheat oven to 325°. Place brisket in roasting pan. Place onions, celery stalks and chili sauce over beef; sprinkle with salt and pepper. Pour water in corner of pan so it seeps to bottom without disturbing meat. Cover tightly with foil; roast 3 1/2 hours. Pour beer over meat; recover; cook 1-1 1/2 hours until tender. Remove meat; cool. Strain juice; chill to remove fat. Slice meat; return juice to meat. Reheat and serve or freeze.

MEAT   Bonnie S. London

Texas Style BBQ Brisket

5	pounds beef brisket	2	tablespoons brown sugar
2	tablespoons liquid smoke	2	teaspoons pepper
1	tablespoon soy sauce	2	teaspoons celery salt
2	teaspoons Worcestershire sauce	1	tablespoon Accent
1	teaspoon minced garlic	1	teaspoon onion salt
1	cup barbeque sauce		

Cut excess fat from brisket. Use a fork to poke several holes in meat to tenderize. Place in deep baking dish; set aside. Mix liquid smoke, soy sauce, Worcestershire sauce, garlic, barbeque sauce, brown sugar, pepper, celery salt, Accent and onion salt in bowl. Pour mixture over brisket. Cover. For best results marinate overnight. Preheat oven to 250°. Bake, covered 5 hours. Drain; slice.

MEAT   Rebecca Robison Ternus

Helene Brenner's Cranberry Brisket

4 pounds brisket
1 cup water
1 (1 ounce) envelope dried onion
   soup

1 (14 ounce) can whole berry
   cranberry sauce

Preheat oven to 325°. Put brisket in oven-safe pan or crock pot; add water. Mix onion soup with cranberry sauce; pour over brisket. Cover; cook in oven 3½ hours or in crock pot on low 8-10 hours.

This recipe is good for chicken too. Put chicken in pan. Fill with water to depth of ½-inch. Use one envelope of soup and one can cranberry sauce for every 4-5 pieces chicken. Cook 350° 1 hour.

Good for times when you don't know what time you're going to serve. Brisket or chicken can be held in the oven until time to serve.

Serves 6

MEAT   *Fern Shinbaum*

Brisket in Wine

5-6 pounds brisket
   Your favorite dry seasonings
2 big onions, sliced

1 cup brown sugar
1 cup white wine

Preheat oven to 350°. Rub brisket with your favorite dry seasonings. Put in foil-lined pan, fat side up. Cook uncovered, 2 hours. Mix brown sugar and wine; set aside. Lower heat to 325°. Cover brisket with onions and wine mixture. Cover; cook 2½ hours.

MEAT   *Sandi Stern*

Brisket by Jeanette

2½-3 pounds beef brisket
1 (1 ounce) package dry onion mushroom soup mix
1½ cups hot water
1 onion, sliced

2 cloves garlic
2 teaspoons salt
1 teaspoon pepper
1 teaspoon Greek seasoning

Preheat oven to 400°. Pat meat dry; put into Dutch oven, fat side up. Brown 30 minutes in oven, uncovered. Mix soup mix with water; stir to dissolve; set aside. Peel and slice onion; peel garlic. Remove meat from oven; lower heat to 325°. Put salt, pepper and Greek seasonings on top of meat. Put onion slices and garlic on top of meat. Pour soup over the top. Cover pan; return to oven. Check for doneness after 20 minutes per pound by inserting fork into thickest part of meat. When meat is done, it will feel soft and tender.

4 to 5 servings per pound

MEAT   Jeanette C. Rousso

Leg of Lamb

1 leg of lamb
1 (1 ounce) envelope dry onion soup mix

Mis Rubin's Black Magic Seasoning
Dale's Steak Sauce to taste
Season salt to taste

Trim fat from lamb. Place in a shallow dish; rub with onion soup mix and Black Magic. Pour Dale's sauce on lamb; sprinkle with season salt. Cover; place in refrigerator overnight. Remove; fully wrap in foil. Grill over indirect heat to 160° on meat thermometer. Take off grill; let sit in foil 30 minutes.

My father, Rubin Hanan, used to make this. For over 50 years he owned a corner grocery specializing in premium meats. He named his original seasonings after our mother Rachel.

MEAT   Rochelle Hanan Koslin

Osso Buco – Lamb or Veal Shank

4-6 lamb or veal shanks
2 onions, chopped
2 cloves garlic, diced
1 green bell pepper
1 cup diced celery
1 (14.5 ounce) can diced tomatoes, drained

1 teaspoon Worcestershire sauce
3 slices of lemon
2 teaspoons basil
2 teaspoons thyme or 1 bay leaf
1/2 cup ketchup
Salt to taste
Pepper to taste

Preheat oven to 325°. Braise shanks in pot or brown on grill. Set aside. Sauté onions and garlic; add bell pepper, celery, tomatoes, Worcestershire sauce, lemon, basil, thyme or bay leaf, ketchup, salt and pepper. Cook 5-10 minutes, until well blended; add shanks. Cover; bake 1 1/2-2 hours, until very tender. Baste every 30 minutes.

MEAT   *Pearl C. Hasson*

Rack of Lamb with Fig-Port Shallot Sauce

4 tablespoons olive oil, divided
2 teaspoons dried rosemary
2 teaspoons dried minced thyme
2 shallots
2 (8-9 chops per rack) frenched racks of lamb

1 cup port wine, divided
8 fresh mission figs or 6 dried figs, cut in quarters
1/2 cup chicken stock

Preheat oven to 450°. In food processor with metal blade, process 2 tablespoons olive oil, rosemary, thyme and shallots 30-45 seconds or until a thick paste forms. Rub herb paste onto lamb. Heat 2 tablespoons oil in medium oven proof skillet. Add lamb, fat side down; cover; cook on high heat 5 minutes on each side to brown. Add 1/2 cup port. Put in oven; roast 18 minutes. Remove lamb; cover with foil. Add remaining 1/2 cup port and figs to skillet; bring to simmer. Add stock; simmer 3-4 minutes until thickened. Pour over lamb and serve.

Serves 4

If you can't find racks of lamb already frenched, with meat cut away from the bones, your butcher should be able to do it for you.

MEAT   *Marie Berlin*

Veal with Mushrooms and Artichoke Hearts

1   (3-4 ounce) fresh veal
     scaloppine
1   egg
1   tablespoon flour
1   tablespoon dry breadcrumbs
     Olive oil as needed
1   shallot, finely chopped

2   medium mushrooms, sliced
1   (14.5 ounce) can artichoke
     hearts, cut into small pieces
¼   cup white wine
     Salt to taste
     Pepper to taste

Preheat oven to 200°. Beat egg; set aside. Combine flour and breadcrumbs; set aside. Dip veal into egg; then dredge in flour mixture. Sauté lightly in olive oil. Keep warm in oven until you make sauce. In the same skillet, sauté shallots until clear. Add mushrooms; sauté 1 minute; add artichokes, wine, salt and pepper; simmer 2 minutes; spoon on top of veal.

You may also use chicken breast pounded very thin, for this recipe. It is delicious.

Serves 1

MEAT   *Corinne F. Capilouto*

Gaena con Enjanadas – Lemon Chicken with Artichokes

2 cloves garlic, coarsely chopped
½ onion, chopped
¼ cup canola oil
1 cup flour
2 tablespoons salt
1 tablespoon pepper
4-6 chicken breasts
1 (6 ounce) jar marinated artichoke hearts

1 (14 ounce) can quartered water-packed artichoke hearts
1 chicken bouillon cube
¾ cup hot water
Juice of 1 lemon
1 tablespoon oregano
2 tablespoons olive oil
1 cup pitted Kalamata olives
Fresh parsley, chopped

Preheat oven to 350°. Cover bottom of 9x13 baking pan with garlic and onion. Heat canola oil in large heavy skillet over medium heat. Put flour into paper bag or shallow pan. Add salt and pepper. Mix together. Dredge chicken pieces in flour mixture. Put chicken in skillet; sauté until browned on all sides, about 10 minutes; transfer to baking pan. Drain marinated artichoke hearts, reserving marinade. Drain water-packed artichoke hearts, discarding liquid. Combine all artichoke hearts in medium bowl; set aside. Crush bouillon cube into water, stir to dissolve. Combine bouillon, reserved marinade, lemon juice, oregano and olive oil; whisk together. Pour mixture into skillet used to brown chicken; thoroughly heat. Pour mixture over chicken. Top with artichoke hearts. Cover; bake 45 minutes, basting every 15 minutes with pan juices. Uncover, top with Kalamata olives; heat until hot and bubbly, about 15 minutes. Top with chopped, fresh parsley.

MEAT   *Sephardic Dinner 2007*

Artichoke Chicken

3	tablespoons margarine	1	cup sliced mushrooms
8	garlic cloves, minced, divided	1	(14 ounce) can artichoke hearts packed in water, drained and quartered
6	boneless, skinless chicken breasts, pounded to an even thickness	2	tablespoons white wine
1	tablespoon olive oil	1	tablespoon fresh lemon juice

Melt margarine in large skillet. Add ½ the garlic; cook 1 minute over medium heat. Add chicken; cook 4-6 minutes per side. Remove to serving platter. Place oil in same skillet. Add remaining garlic; cook 1 minute over medium heat. Add mushrooms; cook 3 minutes. Scrape up brown bits. Add artichokes; cook 1 minute. Add wine and lemon juice; bring to boil. Reduce heat to low; simmer 5 minutes. Pour mushrooms and artichokes over chicken. Serve immediately.

Serves 6

MEAT   *Marie Berlin*

Mediterranean Chicken

1	tablespoon flour	1	green pepper cut into rings
1	tablespoon paprika	1	(8 ounce) carton sliced mushrooms
3-3½	pounds chicken, cut up	¼	cup soy sauce
1	(15 ounce) can artichoke hearts, drained	2	tablespoons wine vinegar
1	medium onion, sliced or chopped	1	clove garlic
			Pinch oregano

Preheat oven to 325°. Place flour and paprika in a gallon size plastic bag. Shake to mix. Add chicken; shake to coat. Remove chicken from flour mixture; place in 9x13 baking dish. Add artichoke hearts, onion, green pepper and mushrooms. Mix together soy sauce, vinegar, garlic and oregano. Pour over chicken. Cover. Bake 45 minutes. Uncover; bake until chicken is lightly browned.

Serves 4 to 6

MEAT   *Bonnie S. London*

Roasted Chicken

1	roasting chicken		Paprika
	Garlic powder	1	cup dark corn syrup

Preheat oven to 350°. Put chicken in roasting pan. Sprinkle outside of chicken with garlic powder and paprika as desired. Cover with loose tent of foil; bake 15 minutes per pound. 30 minutes before end of cooking time, uncover chicken, pour syrup over skin. Increase temperature to 400°. Cook 30 minutes. Save juices for gravy. Just as tasty with turkey.

Great for Rosh Hashanah or anytime!

Serves 6 to 8

MEAT   *Bella Smith*

Chicken and Eggplant Stew

1	pound boneless chicken, cut into 2-inch pieces		Salt to taste
	Your favorite brand chicken seasoning		Pepper to taste
			Dash lemon pepper
2	tablespoons canola oil	2	medium Japanese eggplants, peeled, cut lengthwise, salted
3	onions, thinly sliced		
1½	cups chicken broth or water	2	tablespoons olive oil
1	(6 ounce) can tomato paste		Cooked rice

Coat chicken pieces with chicken seasoning. Heat canola oil in saucepan; add onion; sauté until golden brown. Add chicken; cook until brown. Add broth or water; bring to boil. Lower heat; simmer. Add tomato paste, salt, pepper and lemon pepper. Continue cooking until chicken is tender. Rinse salt off eggplant. In another pan, sauté eggplant in olive oil until golden brown. Place eggplant on top of chicken, but do not stir. Simmer 10 minutes. Serve over rice.

MEAT   *Amy Labovitz*

Lori's Chicken and Eggplant

6 boneless, skinless chicken
    breasts, flattened
    Juice of 2 lemons
2 cloves garlic, crushed
    Dash rosemary
    Dash thyme

    Dash oregano
    Salt to taste
    Pepper to taste
1 eggplant, sliced in ¼-inch slices
    Oil for sautéing
    Butter for sautéing

Preheat oven to 350°. Marinate chicken breasts in lemon juice, garlic, rosemary, thyme, oregano, salt and pepper 45 minutes. Lightly sauté eggplant in oil and butter. Place eggplant slices in 9x13 baking dish. Layer chicken over eggplant. Pour marinade over all. Bake 45 minutes uncovered.

MEAT
Sylvia Capouano

Barbecue Chicken Breasts

½ cup cooking oil
½ cup ketchup
2 tablespoons prepared mustard
¼ cup vinegar
½ cup honey

4 boneless, skinless chicken
    breasts
    Salt to taste
    Pepper to taste

Preheat oven to 350°. Combine oil, ketchup, mustard, vinegar and honey in glass bowl; whisk; set aside. Rinse and dry chicken; season with salt and pepper. Arrange in 8x8 baking pan. Pour sauce over seasoned chicken. Cook covered 15-20 minutes, or until middle of largest breast is light pink. Remove cover; bake 15 minutes.

You may add onions and/or cut up potatoes to chicken and sauce. Use sauce for a roast. You may substitute ½ cup maple syrup for honey for a different taste. Always season meat prior to pouring the sauce over it. Double recipe for more than 5 chicken breasts.

Serves 4

MEAT
Ruby Goldfield

Bar-B-Que Chicken

1	medium size onion, coarsely chopped	3	tablespoons Worcestershire sauce
2	tablespoons + 1 cup vegetable oil	1/2	tablespoon prepared mustard
1/2	cup chopped celery	1	cup ketchup
2	tablespoons brown sugar	1	whole chicken
2	tablespoons lemon juice	1	cup vegetable oil
1/4	cup white vinegar		

Preheat oven to 325°. Brown onion in 2 tablespoons oil. Add celery, brown sugar, lemon juice, vinegar, Worcestershire sauce, mustard and ketchup. Simmer 20 minutes. While sauce simmers, cut chicken into serving pieces. Brown pieces in 1 cup oil; place in 9x13 baking dish. Pour sauce over chicken. Bake uncovered 1 hour.

MEAT   *Rita Rosenthal*

Chicken Piccata

4	chicken cutlets	1	teaspoon minced garlic
	Salt and pepper	1/2	cup chicken broth
	Flour	2	tablespoons fresh lemon juice
2	tablespoons vegetable oil	2	tablespoons butter
1/4	cup dry white wine		Lemon slices

Season chicken cutlets with salt and pepper; dust with flour. Sauté cutlets in oil until brown. Transfer cutlets to warm plate. Pour off fat; deglaze pan with 1/4 cup dry white wine. Add garlic; cook until slightly brown. Add chicken broth and lemon juice. Return cutlets to pan; cook 1 minute on each side. Transfer to warm plate. Add butter and fresh lemon slices to sauce; pour over cutlets.

Serves 4

MEAT   *Diane K. Blondheim*

Belle's Baked Chicken Dish

1   head garlic, peeled
1/3 cup extra virgin olive oil
4-5 large chicken breasts, bone-in
    with skin

1/4 teaspoon, heaping, McCormick's
    Lemon Pepper
1   large onion, coarsely chopped
4   cups canned chicken broth

Mince garlic; combine with olive oil. Rub chicken, over and under skin, thoroughly with garlic mince. Season with lemon pepper. Place in 9x13 pan. Top with chopped onion. Cover; refrigerate overnight. Remove; bring to room temperature. Preheat oven to 425°. Pour 2 cups broth over chicken; place in oven. Brown, then turn; baste chicken every 20 minutes. After browned, reduce heat to 350°. Cook 1½ hours or until golden brown on both sides. Baste and turn as necessary for even cooking. As long as you baste well, it will not be dry. Serve chicken with juices and onion alongside.

This dish freezes well. I recommend freezing chicken and gravy separately.

> *Steve and I think this is the best baked chicken we have ever had...thanks to his sweet mother!*

MEAT   *Samye & Steve Kermish*

Tuscan Chicken

4	boneless, skinless chicken breasts	¼	cup lime juice
	Salt to taste	1	envelope Italian salad dressing mix
	Pepper to taste	¼	cup parve margarine, melted

Preheat oven to 325°. Season chicken with salt and pepper. Place in 9x13 baking dish. Mix lime juice, salad dressing mix and margarine. Pour mixture over chicken. Cover. Bake 45 minutes. Remove cover; continue baking 15 minutes. Serve with brown rice.

Serves 4

MEAT   *Dale B. Evans*

Chicken Breasts with Pine Nuts

4	boneless chicken cutlets	½	cup pine nuts
2	tablespoons parve margarine		Juice of 1 large lemon
1	tablespoon vegetable oil	2	tablespoons white wine, optional
1	large clove garlic, minced	2	scallions, green tops only, chopped

Flatten chicken breasts with meat mallet. In large skillet melt margarine and oil until hot. Add chicken breasts; cook over medium-high heat 2 minutes on each side or until they brown slightly. Remove from skillet. Add garlic and pine nuts to skillet. Cook until pine nuts just begin to brown. Remove skillet from heat, while still hot, add lemon juice and wine, if using. Stir, deglazing pan. Add scallion greens; return chicken to pan. Spoon pine nut mixture over chicken. Cover skillet; cook over low heat 5-10 minutes, until breasts are cooked through, but not overdone!

Serves 4

MEAT   *Helene Krupnick,*
wife of former Agudath Israel Rabbi Aaron Krupnick

Orange and Cashew Chicken

4	(6 ounce) chicken breasts	1	cup toasted cashews or almonds, divided
1/4	cup flour	1	cup orange juice
1	teaspoon salt	3	cups cooked rice
1/4	cup vegetable oil		

Cut chicken into bite size pieces. Mix flour with salt; lightly dust chicken. In a large skillet sauté chicken and 1/2 cup nuts in oil until golden brown. Add orange juice. Cover; cook on low heat 20 minutes. Uncover, remove chicken to serving dish. Reduce liquid to a thickened sauce. Pour sauce over chicken, sprinkle with remaining nuts; serve over rice.

Serves 6

MEAT   *Rebecca Robinson Ternus*

Roasted Rosemary Chicken

1	(3 1/2 pound) chicken, cut into pieces	1	tablespoon minced garlic
2	tablespoons olive oil	1	sprig fresh rosemary, finely minced
1	onion, slivered or sliced		Salt to taste
1	(8 ounce) carton fresh mushrooms, sliced		Pepper to taste
		2/3	cup prepared marinara sauce
		1/2	cup water

Preheat oven to 375°. Arrange chicken in shallow roasting pan. Sauté onion and mushrooms in olive oil 5 minutes, add garlic; sauté 5 minutes. Add minced rosemary. Toss chicken with onion mixture; season with salt and pepper. Top with marinara sauce. Pour water into bottom of pan. Bake 1 hour or until chicken is cooked through. Spoon sauce over chicken before serving.

Serves 6

MEAT   *Bonnie S. London*

Aunt Evelyn's Potato Chip Chicken

Cooking spray
1 (10 ounce) bag potato chips per
   10 chicken pieces
1 whole chicken, cut up, or your
   favorite pre-cut pieces

¼ cup oil, any kind
   Garlic powder to taste
   Paprika to taste

Preheat oven to 350°. Spray roasting pan with cooking spray. Crush potato chips in plastic bag. Clean chicken; pat dry. Coat each piece with oil. Season all sides with garlic powder and paprika. Shake chicken pieces in bag of crushed chips until well covered. Place in roasting pan skin side up. Add more garlic powder and paprika if desired. Cover chicken with remaining crushed chips. Roast uncovered 1½ hours.

Serves 4

We had this chicken for Passover many, many years ago in Denver at the home of Eddie's aunt and uncle, Evelyn and Richard Saliman. We could not stop eating it. The potato chips keep the chicken really moist. Buy a few extra bags for crushing on top...and for eating while you cook. Yum!

MEAT

Lanie & Eddie Raymon

Chicken and Sun-Dried Tomatoes over Fettuccine

4　chicken breast halves, skinned
　　and boned

1　(7 ounce) jar sun-dried tomatoes
　　in oil

½　cup chopped onion

2　cloves garlic, minced

2　tablespoons snipped fresh basil
　　or 2 teaspoons dried basil

¼　cup sliced ripe olives, optional

2　tablespoons capers

2　tablespoons olive oil

½　teaspoon salt

¼　teaspoon pepper

¼　teaspoon crushed red pepper

8　ounces fettuccine

Cut chicken into ½-inch strips, set aside. Drain sun-dried tomatoes, reserving oil. Coarsely chop tomatoes; set aside. In 12-inch skillet, heat 1 tablespoon reserved oil over medium heat. Add onion and garlic; cook until tender. Add chicken; cook 8 minutes or until tender, stirring occasionally. Add basil and tomatoes, cook 1 more minute. Stir in olives, capers, olive oil, salt, pepper, red pepper and 2 tablespoons of reserved oil from tomatoes; heat through. Meanwhile, cook pasta in boiling salted water until tender but still firm. Drain well. Return pasta to pot, add chicken mixture; toss well.

Serves 4

MEAT　　　　　　　　　　　　　　　　　　　　　　　Robin Blitz

Chicken Spaghetti

6	boneless chicken breasts	1/2	teaspoon salt
	Olive oil	1/2	teaspoon pepper
1	large chopped onion	1/2	teaspoon basil
3	stalks celery, chopped	1/2	teaspoon oregano
1	(14.5 ounce) can diced tomatoes	1/2	teaspoon thyme
2	cups chicken broth	1	pound spaghetti
1	(6 ounce) can tomato paste		

Brown chicken in olive oil until golden. Set aside. In large Dutch oven, cook onions and celery until transparent. Add tomatoes, chicken broth, tomato paste, salt, pepper, basil, oregano and thyme. Slice chicken; add to sauce. Cook 15-20 minutes. Meanwhile, cook spaghetti according to package directions. Toss chicken sauce and spaghetti together. Serve immediately.

MEAT   Sandi Stern

Chicken or Veal Piccata

4	chicken or veal cutlets	1/4	cup dry white wine
	Salt to taste	1	teaspoon minced garlic
	Pepper to taste	1/2	cup chicken broth
2	tablespoons flour	2	tablespoons fresh lemon juice
2	tablespoons vegetable oil		

Season cutlets with salt and pepper; dust with flour. Sauté in oil until brown. Transfer to warm plate. Pour off fat; deglaze pan with wine. Add garlic. Cook until garlic is slightly brown. Add broth and lemon juice. Return cutlets to pan; cook 1 minute on each side. Transfer cutlets to serving plate. Serve immediately.

MEAT   Diane Blondheim

Chicken Cacciatore

1 pound boneless, skinless chicken breast
¼ cup flour
¾ teaspoon salt, divided
⅜ teaspoon pepper, divided
3 tablespoons vegetable oil
1 (6 ounce) jar marinated artichoke hearts
1 tablespoon olive oil
½ medium onion, diced

1 medium carrot, diced
½ medium green bell pepper, diced
1 stalk celery, diced
¼ pound mushrooms, sliced
2 cloves garlic, minced
1 (28 ounce) can Italian tomatoes
½ teaspoon dried oregano
1 teaspoon dried basil
1 medium bay leaf
⅛ teaspoon crushed red pepper

Preheat oven to 350°. Cut chicken into cubes; dredge in flour. Season with ¼ teaspoon salt and ⅛ teaspoon pepper. Heat vegetable oil in large skillet over medium-high heat; brown chicken. Remove from skillet; wipe skillet clean. Drain artichoke hearts, reserving marinade. Coarsely chop artichokes. Heat olive oil and reserved marinade in skillet over medium heat. Sauté onion, carrot, bell pepper, celery, mushrooms and garlic 5 minutes. Add tomatoes with juice, artichoke hearts, oregano, basil, bay leaf, red pepper flakes, ½ teaspoon salt and ¼ teaspoon pepper. Simmer 10 minutes, partially covered. Lay chicken in 9x13 baking dish. Pour vegetable sauce over chicken; cover tightly with foil; bake 30 minutes. Serve with pasta or rice.

Freezes well.

Serves 4

MEAT   *Nick G. Ashner*

Fish in Parmesan Herb Breading

1	medium lemon	1/8	teaspoon salt
2	tablespoons butter, softened	1/4	teaspoon Italian seasoning
3	tablespoons capers, rinsed	3/4	pound fresh fish
1/2	cup grated Parmesan cheese	1	large egg white
1/8	cup dry breadcrumbs		

Preheat oven to 425°. Cut lemon in half; make one thin slice for garnish; set aside. Zest lemon; then juice. Mix zest and juice with softened butter; gently stir in capers. Place in small container; store in refrigerator. Mix Parmesan cheese, breadcrumbs, salt and Italian seasonings; set aside. Wash and dry fish thoroughly. Whip egg white until frothy. Immediately dip dry fish in egg white; then coat with Parmesan herb breading. Place coated fish in baking pan. Bake uncovered, approximately 12 minutes per inch of thickness, at thickest part of fish. If less than 1-inch thick, adjust time accordingly. Do not overcook. Fish is done when just a hint of translucence is seen when cut into thickest part of fish. Fish will continue to cook after being removed from heat and will lose that hint of translucence. Overcooked fish will be dry and tough. Plate fish. Top with butter and capers mixture. Serve immediately.

Serves 2

DAIRY   *Nick G. Ashner*

Suit Yourself Fish Taco Bar

1   pound package frozen tilapia, thawed
Juice of 1 large lime
Salt
Pepper
1   medium onion, cut in thin strips
1   small green pepper, cut in thin strips
1   small red pepper, cut in thin strips
1   small yellow or orange pepper, cut in thin strips

Olive oil cooking spray
1/2   cup pineapple tidbits
1   cup chopped fresh tomato
1   cup lettuce, chopped in small strips
3/4   cup grated Cheddar cheese
1   cup sour cream
1/2   cup salsa
Sliced jalapeños
8   whole wheat tortilla wraps

Preheat oven to broil. Coat 11x7 baking dish with cooking spray; place fish in dish. Squeeze lime juice over fish. Sprinkle with salt and lots of pepper. Broil about 5-7 minutes on each side until fish flakes with fork. Break fish into small chunks; transfer to serving bowl; set aside; keep warm. Spray onion and peppers with cooking spray; sauté until tender-crisp. Transfer to separate serving bowl; keep warm. Put pineapple, tomato, lettuce, cheese, sour cream, salsa and jalapeños in small dishes and tortilla wraps on a plate. Arrange all dishes on a self-serve bar and enjoy!

Serves 4

DAIRY

Dale B. Evans

Baked Halibut with Artichokes

1   (6 ounce) jar marinated artichoke
    hearts
1   (14 ounce) can stewed tomatoes
½   teaspoon dried oregano

½   teaspoon onion salt
⅛   tablespoon fresh parsley, minced
2   (6 ounce) halibut fillets
½   cup grated Parmesan cheese

Preheat oven to 400°. Drain artichoke hearts, reserving marinade. Cut artichokes in half; remove tough leaves. Place reserved marinade in small saucepan with tomatoes, oregano and onion salt. Bring to boil; lower heat; simmer 15 minutes. Add artichoke hearts and parsley. Remove from heat. Place halibut filets in baking dish; pour tomato mixture on top. Bake, uncovered approximately 25-30 minutes. Place on dinner plates; garnish with Parmesan cheese.

Serves 2

DAIRY   *Nick G. Ashner*

Baked Roughy

1½ pounds orange roughy fillets,
    any white fish will work
1   tablespoon lime juice
3   tablespoons mayonnaise
1   teaspoon garlic salt
½   teaspoon black pepper

½   cup Italian breadcrumbs
1½ tablespoons melted butter or
    margarine, may substitute olive
    oil cooking spray
2   tablespoons chopped parsley

Preheat oven to 425°. Spray 11x7 baking dish with cooking spray. Place fish in dish. Drizzle lime juice over fish. In small bowl combine mayonnaise, garlic salt and black pepper; spread over fish. Sprinkle with breadcrumbs. Drizzle with melted butter or spray with olive oil cooking spray. Bake 20 minutes or until fish flakes easily when tested with a fork. Sprinkle with parsley.

Serves 4

DAIRY OR PARVE   *Dale B. Evans*

Asian Salmon

4	serving-size pieces salmon	1	tablespoon soy sauce
	Salt	4	teaspoons Chinese hot mustard
	Pepper	1	teaspoon rice vinegar
3	tablespoons dark brown sugar		

Preheat oven to 425°. Season salmon with salt and pepper, to taste. Bake 12 minutes. While salmon bakes, bring brown sugar, soy sauce, mustard and rice vinegar to boil in small saucepan. Boil 1 minute. Remove salmon from oven; turn on broiler. Brush sauce on salmon. Place salmon under hot broiler 3-5 minutes.

Serves 4

PARVE   Dana Handmacher

Grilled Salmon

1½	pounds salmon fillets	⅓	cup soy sauce
	Lemon pepper to taste	⅓	cup brown sugar
	Garlic powder to taste	⅓	cup water
	Salt to taste	¼	cup vegetable oil

Season salmon with lemon pepper, garlic powder and salt. In small bowl, stir together soy sauce, brown sugar, water and vegetable oil until sugar is dissolved. Place fish and soy sauce mixture in large zip-close plastic bag; seal; turn to coat. Refrigerate at least 2 hours. Preheat grill to medium heat. Lightly oil grill grate. Place fish on grill; discard marinade. Cook 6-8 minutes per side or until fish flakes easily with a fork.

Serves 6

PARVE   Susan Bruchis

Roasted Salmon Niçoise Platter

8 lemons

½ cup olive oil

½ cup + 2 teaspoons Dijon mustard, divided

8 garlic cloves, minced

3 tablespoons + 2 teaspoons kosher salt, divided

3 tablespoons freshly ground black pepper, divided

½ a whole fresh salmon, filleted, skin on

3 pounds small Yukon gold potatoes

1½ pounds French green beans, stems removed

½ cup champagne vinegar

1 cup olive oil, choose good quality

8 small ripe tomatoes, cut into wedges

12 hard-cooked eggs, peeled, cut in ½ lengthwise

1 can anchovies, optional

Arugula, watercress or mixed spring greens for garnish

Preheat oven to 500°. For marinade, zest and juice lemons into glass bowl. Add olive oil, ½ cup mustard, garlic, 3 tablespoons salt and 2 tablespoons pepper; whisk until well blended; set aside. Place salmon in glass baking dish; pour marinade over salmon; spread to moisten entire fish. Cover; rest 15 minutes. Steam potatoes over boiling water until tender, but still firm. When cooled, slice in thick slices; set aside. Bake salmon uncovered 12-15 minutes, until almost cooked through. Transfer to a plate; cool 15 minutes. Remove skin; break into large pieces; set aside. Bring large pot of salted water to rolling boil; add green beans; boil exactly 1½ minutes. Remove from heat; immediately immerse beans in ice water 2 minutes; drain; set aside. For vinaigrette, combine vinegar, 2 teaspoons mustard, 2 teaspoons salt and 1 tablespoon pepper. Slowly whisk in olive oil until completely incorporated; set aside. Arrange salmon, green beans, tomato, eggs and anchovies, if used, on a large platter. Garnish generously with salad greens. Drizzle some vinaigrette over all; serve remainder on the side.

Can be served warm, at room temperature or chilled. A great fix-ahead dinner for the bridge or bunco group. Makes a spectacular display for a brunch, too.

PARVE   *Rhonda Blitz*

Salmon Burgers

1   large clove garlic, peeled
¼   of an onion
1   pound fresh salmon, skin and
      bone removed, cut into chunks
      Juice of 1 lemon
2   tablespoons cocktail sauce
1   egg

6   tablespoons breadcrumbs,
      divided, extra for breading
½   teaspoon salt
¼   teaspoon freshly ground black
      pepper
2   tablespoons canola oil

Chop garlic in food processor. Add onion; process briefly until coarsely chopped. Add salmon; process to a coarse texture similar to ground beef. Remove salmon-onion mixture to bowl. Add lemon juice, cocktail sauce, egg, 2 tablespoons breadcrumbs, salt and pepper; mix thoroughly. Divide mixture into 4 equal parts. Moisten hands with cold water; roll each portion into smooth ball. Flatten each ball into 1-inch thick patty. Bread burgers lightly on each side with breadcrumbs. Heat oil in large skillet over medium heat; cook burgers 3 minutes on each side, or until lightly browned. Serve on toasted sesame seed buns. Spread with cocktail sauce, lettuce and tomato.

Serves 4

PARVE   *Amy Labovitz*

Sweet Barbeque Salmon

4   (6 ounce) salmon fillets
½   cup soy sauce
2   tablespoons honey

1   tablespoon Dijon mustard
1   tablespoon minced fresh parsley
2-3   garlic cloves, minced

Pierce salmon several times with fork; place in sealable plastic bag. Combine soy sauce, honey, mustard, parsley and garlic in bowl; mix well. Reserve 2-3 tablespoons for basting; pour remainder over salmon; seal tightly; turn to coat. Marinate in refrigerator several hours turning occasionally. Grill over medium-high heat 5 minutes each side until fillets flake easily, basting with reserved sauce.

Serves 4

PARVE   *Robin Blitz*

Sweet Bourbon Salmon

1/2	cup pineapple juice	1/4	teaspoon black pepper, cracked
2	tablespoons soy sauce	1/2	teaspoon garlic powder
2	tablespoons brown sugar	1/2	cup vegetable oil
1 1/2	tablespoons bourbon whiskey	2	(8 ounce) salmon fillets, skinned

Whisk juice, soy sauce, brown sugar, bourbon, pepper, garlic powder and oil. Rinse salmon; pat dry. Place salmon in 1-quart zipper plastic bag. Pour marinade in bag with salmon. Marinate minimum one hour. Grill or broil approximately six minutes on each side, until center of fish just starts to cook.

Serves 2

PARVE   *Nick G. Ashner*

Baked Snapper with Potatoes, Oregano & White Wine

3	russet potatoes, peeled, cut into 1/4-inch thick rounds	3/4	cup dry white wine
1/2	cup olive oil, divided	1/4	cup water
3	garlic cloves, minced	4	(5-6 ounce) 3/4-inch thick red snapper fillets
1	teaspoon dried oregano		Salt to taste
1	teaspoon salt		Pepper to taste
1/4	teaspoon dried crushed red pepper flakes	4	tablespoons chopped fresh parsley

Preheat oven to 450°. Slightly overlap sliced potatoes in 9x13 baking dish. Mix 1/4 cup oil, garlic, oregano, salt and red pepper in small bowl. Spread over potatoes. Pour wine and water over potatoes. Cover; bake 20 minutes. Uncover; bake until potatoes are tender, about 35 minutes. Place fish on top of potatoes. Drizzle with remaining 1/4 cup oil. Sprinkle with salt, pepper and parsley. Bake uncovered until fish is opaque in center, about 18-20 minutes. Sprinkle with remaining parsley and serve.

Serves 4

PARVE   *Robin Blitz*

Rebbetzin Irene's Enchiladas

½ cup chili powder
½ teaspoon cumin powder
¼ cup flour
1½ cups cold water
24 tortillas

2 pounds medium Cheddar cheese, grated
Cooking spray
Chopped olives, chopped green onions, chopped green chiles, optional

Preheat oven to 350°. Preheat skillet to 300° or medium heat. Brown chili powder and cumin until it turns slightly darker. Add flour; cook until flour is light brown. Watch closely, it burns easily. Slowly add cold water a little at a time until sauce starts to boil. Continue to add water until sauce is thick enough to stick to tortilla, the consistency of gravy. If too thick, it clumps to the tortilla, too thin, it slides off. If too thin, make a paste of 2 tablespoons flour and 2 tablespoons water; stir until all flour is mixed in. Add paste to sauce 1 teaspoon at a time until it thickens; set aside. Spray clean skillet with cooking spray; heat to 300° or medium heat. Fry each tortilla 10-20 seconds on each side. Recoat with cooking spray as needed. This step can be skipped, but it adds texture and helps maintain consistency.

Spray 9x13 baking dish with cooking spray. Set aside 1 cup cheese. Make an assembly line of tortillas, sauce, empty dinner plate, cheese and baking dish. Take a tortilla with tongs; dip it in sauce. Make sure both sides are covered with sauce. Don't worry about the part in the tongs; use that side to start rolling. Place tortilla on empty plate; add a row of cheese to middle. Spread olives, onions and/or chiles, if using. Roll tortilla; place in baking dish. Continue, using all ingredients. Pour any remaining sauce over top. Cover with aluminum foil. Bake 15 minutes; remove foil; cover with reserved cheese, if you wish; bake uncovered 5-10 minutes, until cheese is melted.

Makes 24 enchiladas

DAIRY

Irene E. Kramer

Eggplant Parmesan

1   large or 2 small eggplant
    Salt
3   eggs, beaten
3   cups Italian breadcrumbs,
    divided
    Vegetable oil and canola oil for
    frying, ½ and ½

2-3 cups your favorite red sauce
3   cups shredded mozzarella
    cheese
2   cups grated Parmesan/Romano
    cheese

Preheat oven to 350°. Peel eggplant; cut in ¼-inch slices; salt. Let sit 10-15 minutes; pat dry. Put up to 2¾ cups breadcrumbs in dish. Dip eggplant in egg, then breadcrumbs; fry in oil. Layer bottom of greased 9x13 glass baking dish with ½ of eggplant; add ½ of red sauce. Top with ½ of mozzarella, then ½ of Parmesan/Romano. Add second layer of eggplant, red sauce, mozzarella and Parmesan/Romano. Top with ¼ cup breadcrumbs. Bake 20-25 minutes.

Eat. Save leftovers. Eat again the next day.

DAIRY   *Bill Raymon*

Italian Stuffed Shells

1   (12 ounce) box jumbo shells
32 ounces ricotta cheese
16 ounces Four Italian Cheese mix,
    shredded
1   egg

2   tablespoons parsley, chopped
52 ounces spaghetti sauce
6   ounces mozzarella cheese,
    shredded

Preheat oven to 350°. Cook shells in boiling water until barely tender. Drain; let cool. Combine ricotta cheese, cheese mix, egg and parsley. Cover bottom of 9x13 baking dish with spaghetti sauce. Fill shells with cheese mixture. Place in baking dish. Cover shells with remaining spaghetti sauce. Top with mozzarella cheese. Cover with foil. Bake 35 minutes or until hot and bubbly.

Freezes well.

DAIRY   *Rebecca Robison Ternus*

Mac & Cheese

1 (8 ounce) package elbow macaroni

1 (10.75 ounce) can condensed Cheddar cheese soup

1/2 cup milk

3 cups shredded sharp Cheddar cheese, divided

1 egg, beaten

1 tablespoon butter

1/2 teaspoon salt, optional

1/4 teaspoon black pepper

Preheat oven to 375°. Coat oven-proof bowl with cooking spray. Cook macaroni according to package directions. Drain; pour into prepared bowl. Stir in soup, milk, 2³/₄ cups cheese, egg, butter, salt and pepper. Sprinkle with reserved 1/4 cup cheese. Bake 12-20 minutes, until liquid is absorbed and top is lightly browned. Cool 5 minutes. Serve and enjoy.

Can be baked in muffin tins for individual servings.

DAIRY   *Nomie Sharker*

World's Greatest Crock Pot Mac and Cheese

Non-stick cooking spray

1 (8 ounce) box elbow macaroni

1 (15 ounce) can evaporated milk

1 cup whole milk

2 cups shredded sharp Cheddar cheese

2 cups shredded mild Cheddar cheese, divided

2 eggs

1/2 cup butter

Dash salt

Pepper to taste

Coat crock pot generously with cooking spray. Cook macaroni according to directions on box. DO NOT OVERCOOK. Combine evaporated milk, whole milk, sharp Cheddar, 1 cup mild Cheddar, eggs, butter, salt and pepper with cooked macaroni. Transfer to crock pot. Top mixture with remaining cup mild Cheddar. DO NOT STIR. Cook on low 3¹/₂ to 4 hours.

Serves 8

DAIRY   *Leslie Capp*

Vegetarian Lasagna Rolls

2   tablespoons olive or vegetable oil
2   carrots, finely chopped
1/3 cup finely chopped onion
1   (10 ounce) package frozen chopped broccoli, thawed, drained
1/2 teaspoon salt
1/8 teaspoon pepper

8   lasagna noodles
1 3/4 cups shredded provolone cheese, divided
1   cup ricotta or cottage cheese
1   egg, lightly beaten
1/2 cup tomato sauce or spaghetti sauce

Preheat oven to 350°. Heat oil in medium skillet over medium-high heat; add carrots and onion. Cook 5 minutes, stirring constantly. Add broccoli, salt and pepper; cook 10 minutes. Meanwhile, cook lasagna noodles according to package directions. Drain; rinse under cold water; set aside. Stir in 1 cup provolone cheese, ricotta or cottage cheese and egg into vegetable mixture. Spread 1/4 cup tomato or spaghetti sauce in 8x8 baking dish. Spread 1 noodle flat on work surface; cut in half cross-wise. Spread 1/3 cup filling on each piece; roll up. Place rolls, seam side down, in the dish. Cover rolls with remaining sauce. Cover; bake 30 minutes. Uncover; sprinkle remaining provolone cheese over rolls; bake uncovered 15 minutes.

DAIRY   Susan Bruchis

Tofu Pasta

¼ cup tamari sauce

¼ cup toasted sesame oil

3 tablespoons hot sesame oil, divided

2-4 tablespoons sesame seeds, toasted

Juice of 1 lime

½ teaspoon black pepper

½ teaspoon garlic powder

½ teaspoon dry mustard

1 pound firm tofu, cut in ¾-inch pieces

1 pound green fettuccini or pasta of your choice

1 bunch scallions, trimmed and chopped

1 red bell pepper, cut into match stick pieces

Combine tamari sauce, toasted sesame oil, 2 tablespoons hot sesame oil, sesame seeds, lime juice, pepper, garlic powder and mustard. Marinate tofu chunks at least 1 hour in mixture. Cook pasta to al dente; drain well. Toss pasta with 1 tablespoon hot pepper sesame oil. Add tofu mixture, scallions and bell pepper to pasta. Voila! Serve warm.

Serves 4

PARVE *Goldie Knurr*

Zucchini Chimichangas

½ cup oil, divided

5 zucchini, diced

1 (4 ounce) can green chili, diced

¾ cup diced onion

1¾ teaspoons dried oregano

1½ teaspoons cumin

¾ cup crushed tortilla chips

¼ cup minced cilantro

6 ounces Monterey Jack cheese, grated

Salt to taste

8 flour tortillas

1 (8 ounce) container sour cream

1 (8 ounce) jar salsa

Preheat oven to 425°. Heat 3 tablespoons oil in large skillet over medium high heat; add zucchini, chili, onion, oregano and cumin. Sauté 10 minutes or just until vegetables are tender. Remove from heat; let cool slightly. Stir in tortilla chips, cilantro, cheese and salt. Spray baking sheet with cooking spray. Divide zucchini mixture among tortillas. Fold sides to center; roll up from open end. Lay filled tortillas, seam-side down, on baking sheet. Use remaining oil as needed to brush tops and sides of each roll. Bake 15-20 minutes, until golden brown and crisp. Serve with sour cream and salsa.

DAIRY *Nick G. Ashner*

Vegetable Pot Pie with Sherry Cream Sauce

2³/₄ cups flour, divided

1 teaspoon salt

1¹/₂ tablespoons fresh dill, minced

¹/₂ cup and 4 tablespoons butter, chilled, divided

7-8 tablespoons ice water

1 medium red onion, diced

1 cup vegetable stock

³/₄ cup half-and-half, heated

2 teaspoons fresh rosemary, minced

1 teaspoon dried savory, crumbled

¹/₂ teaspoon salt

¹/₄ teaspoon white pepper

2 tablespoons dry sherry

3 stalks celery, diced

2 medium carrots, diced

1 (8 ounce) carton mushrooms, diced

1 cup corn kernels

1 cup frozen peas, thawed

1 egg yolk

Preheat oven to 400°. To make crust, sift together 2¹/₄ cups flour and salt in medium bowl. Stir in dill. Cut in ¹/₂ cup butter with pastry cutter. Add ice water, 1 tablespoon at a time as needed for dough to form but not be sticky. Cover with plastic wrap; chill until ready to use. To make filling, melt 4 tablespoons butter in large skillet over medium heat. Add onion; cook until soft. Whisk in ¹/₂ cup flour; cook, stirring constantly, 2 minutes. Add vegetable stock, half-and-half, rosemary, savory, salt and pepper; whisk until blended. Stir in sherry, celery, carrots, mushrooms, corn and peas. Partially cover; simmer 8 minutes or until vegetables are tender and sauce is thickened. Remove from heat; divide mixture evenly into 2 pie plates. Divide dough into 2 equal portions. Roll out dough; cover top of pie pans; trim to ¹/₂-inch beyond plate edge. Use fingers to seal and flute edges. Beat egg yolk with a little water; brush over dough; cut steam vents. Place in freezer at least 20 minutes. Remove from freezer, bake uncovered 45 minutes. Cover with foil if crust starts to get too brown.

Serves 8

DAIRY

Nick G. Ashner

Complements...

...to enjoy from generation to generation!

Breads
Rice & Grains
Vegetables

You've got the main course down pat —
now serve up side dishes to take your meal from ordinary
to awesome. Choose from these recipes for breads, potatoes,
rice and veggies to enhance the flavors of your entrée.

Gramma Jeanna's Whole Wheat Bread Recipe

1 egg	1 teaspoon salt
1½ cups lukewarm water	3 cups whole wheat flour, not coarse ground
2½ tablespoons olive oil	
3 tablespoons dry milk	1½ cups Pillsbury bread flour
7 tablespoons sugar	4½ teaspoons Rapid Rise Yeast

Place egg, water and olive oil in bread machine. Add dry milk, sugar, salt and flours. Add yeast on top. Mix to a sticky dough. Roll marble size piece of dough in hand. If too dry, add more water 1 tablespoon at a time. If too sticky, add more flour 1 tablespoon at a time. Set machine on rise 1-1½ hours. Remove dough from bread machine to counter. For 2 loaves, make 6 balls. Cover; let rest 15 minutes. Shape into ropes. Dust with flour; braid. Place in wax paper lined loaf pans. Cover; let rise 1-1½ hours. Preheat oven to 360°. Before baking, carefully brush with beaten egg; sprinkle with sesame seeds. Bake 30-35 minutes. Remove from oven. Invert on kitchen towel. Remove wax paper carefully. Cool on wire racks. When completely cool, store in bread bags.

DAIRY   *Leon Capouano*

Sour Cream Biscuits

2 cups self-rising flour	1 (8 ounce) carton sour cream
1 cup melted butter	

Preheat oven to 400°. Mix flour, butter and sour cream just until incorporated. Drop into UNGREASED muffin tins. Bake 12-15 minutes. Cool on wire rack.

DAIRY   *Barbara Handmacher*

Leon Capouano's Challah Bread

2	eggs	2	tablespoons dry milk
1¼	cups milk	1	teaspoon salt
4	tablespoons olive oil	4½	cups bread flour
5	tablespoons sugar	4	teaspoons Rapid Rise Yeast

Place eggs, milk and olive oil in bread machine or electric mixer. Add dry milk, salt and flour. Add yeast on top. Mix to a slightly sticky dough, should feel like a baby's tush. Test marble size piece of dough by rolling in your hand. If too sticky add more flour. Set machine on rise 1 hour. For mixer, use bread dough hook; mix on medium speed. Scrape sides with spatula. Mix 10-15 minutes. Remove from mixer; place in large bowl. Cover; allow dough to double in size, about 1 hour. Remove dough from bread machine or mixer bowl to counter. Knead 5 minutes; shape into 4 balls. Cover; let rest 15 minutes. Shape into ropes; dust with flour; braid. Place on baking pan or stone, dusted with corn meal. Cover; let rise 1-1½ hours. Preheat oven to 360°. Before baking, gently brush top and sides of bread with beaten egg; sprinkle with poppy seeds or sesame seeds. Bake 30-35 minutes. Remove from oven. Use spatula to remove bread from pan. Cool on wire rack.

To freeze, wrap cooled challah in aluminum foil and place in plastic bag.

1 large loaf

DAIRY   *Leon Capouano*

Ruth Segall's Challah Bread

¹⁄₄ cup and 1 teaspoon sugar, divided	1 teaspoon salt
¹⁄₂ cup warm water	¹⁄₃ cup oil
1 package yeast	2 eggs
3 cups bread flour	¹⁄₄ cup lukewarm water
¹⁄₄ cup sugar	1 egg yolk, beaten with 1 teaspoon water

Mix 1 teaspoon sugar, ¹⁄₄ cup water and yeast. Dissolve yeast well. Mix flour, ¹⁄₄ cup sugar and salt. Put flour mixture in bowl of food processor using metal blade. Pour yeast mixture over flour mixture; process 12-15 seconds. Mix eggs, oil and ¹⁄₄ cup lukewarm water. Add to processor; beat 30 seconds. Knead dough 1-2 minutes. Place in greased bowl; let rest 1 hour. Preheat oven to 325°. Separate dough into three equal parts. Braid; put on greased cookie sheet. Let dough rise again. Brush with egg yolk mixture; bake 30-35 minutes.

> Growing up my mother made this regularly. Not only did we have this for Shabbat dinner, but she would make challah rolls to serve every night. Also, she cheerfully 'distributed' the challah rolls to neighbors and friends.

PARVE   Hazel & Janice Segall

Sweet Shabbat Challah

1½ cups warm water
½ cup honey
1 tablespoon oil
4 eggs and 2 yokes, divided
1½ teaspoons salt
1 tablespoon sugar
3 tablespoons instant active dry yeast
5 cups and several tablespoons flour
2 teaspoons water
Sesame seeds, optional

Combine water, honey, oil, 4 eggs, salt, sugar and yeast in large mixing bowl. Add 5 cups flour; mix until uniform consistency. Continue adding flour, 1 tablespoon at a time until dough is still sticky but comes off your hand without leaving any dough behind. Knead 10 minutes. Place dough in greased bowl; let rise until doubled in volume, 1-1½ hours. Preheat oven to 325°. Punch down dough; knead 1 minute and split in half. Braid each half into challah shape using your favorite method! Place both on greased baking sheet, allowing room for each to expand. Let rise 25-30 minutes. Mix 2 egg yolks with 2 teaspoons water; spread over challah. Add sesame seeds if desired. Bake 30-40 minutes or until done. Let cool and serve with spirit!

To use non-instant active dry yeast, mix yeast, ½ cup water and 1 tablespoon sugar about 10 minutes before mixing it with other ingredients. Be careful; once yeast starts to activate, this mixture will get foamy. Mix with a spoon to keep foam down.

PARVE   *Joel Kramer, son of Rabbi Scott and Rebbetzin Irene Kramer*

Onion Crackers by Ruth Segall

2 large onions, grated
½ cup + 2 tablespoons oil
1 teaspoon salt
¼ teaspoon black pepper
2¼-2½ cups flour
Garlic to taste

Preheat oven to 350°. Mix onions, oil, salt, pepper and flour together into a dough. Shape into walnut size balls; flatten each to cracker shape; place on cookie sheet. Bake 30 minutes; let dry out.

The thinner the dough, the crispier and better the cracker.

PARVE   *Hazel & Janice Segall*

Banana Bread

½	cup butter	1	teaspoon soda
1	cup sugar		Pinch of salt
2	eggs	½	cup chopped nuts
1½	cups flour	3	ripe bananas, mashed

Preheat oven to 350°. Cream butter and sugar 2 minutes, add eggs; beat well. Sift flour, soda and salt together. Add to batter; mix well. Stir in nuts and bananas. Pour into greased and floured loaf pan. Bake 40-50 minutes.

DAIRY   *Clara Berns*

Banana Tea Loaf

1½	cups flour	1	cup mashed, very ripe bananas
½	teaspoon salt	½	cup sour cream or ¼ cup buttermilk
1	teaspoon baking soda		
½	cup butter	½	cup chopped nuts
1	cup sugar	1	cup fresh blueberries or 1 cup chocolate chips, optional
2	eggs		
1	teaspoon vanilla	1	tablespoon flour for coating blueberries, optional

Preheat oven to 350°. Grease 9x5x3 loaf pan; set aside. Combine flour, salt and baking soda; set aside. Cream butter and sugar. Add eggs and vanilla. Add bananas and sour cream or buttermilk. Beat until combined. Mix in dry ingredients; beat ½ minute until blended. If using blueberries, coat them with flour to prevent berries from sinking to pan bottom. If using, stir in blueberries or chocolate chips. Pour into prepared loaf pan; bake 1 hour.

1 loaf

DAIRY   *Toby Gewant*

Marsha's Banana Tea Bread

½ cup butter or margarine, softened

1⅓ cups sugar

2 eggs

¼ cup sour cream or vanilla Greek yogurt

2 tablespoons milk

1 teaspoon almond extract

2 cups flour

1½ cups baking powder

½ teaspoon baking soda

¼ teaspoon salt

1 cup mashed bananas

1½ cups chopped walnuts

¾ cup dark chocolate chips, optional

Preheat oven to 350°. Combine butter or margarine and sugar in large mixing bowl; cream until light and fluffy. Add eggs. Add yogurt or sour cream, milk and almond extract; mix well. Combine flour, baking powder, baking soda and salt; add to creamed mixture alternately with mashed bananas. Mix well after each addition. Stir in nuts. If using, stir in chocolate chips. Pour batter into loaf pan. Bake 1 hour 10 minutes or until done.

DAIRY *Marsha Orange*

Cranberry Poppy Seed Bread

2½ cups all-purpose flour

1 cup sugar

2 tablespoons poppy seeds

1 tablespoon baking powder

¾ cup milk

⅓ cup margarine

2 eggs

1 teaspoon vanilla

2 teaspoons grated lemon peel

1 cup fresh or frozen cranberries, puréed

Preheat oven to 350°. In large bowl, mix flour, sugar, poppy seeds and baking powder; set aside. Blend milk, margarine, eggs, vanilla and lemon peel; stir into flour mixture until moistened. Stir in cranberries. Spread into greased loaf pan. Bake 1 hour.

DAIRY *Sandi Stern*

Pear Bread

½ cup butter	½ teaspoon baking powder
1 cup sugar	⅛ teaspoon nutmeg
2 eggs	¼ cup yogurt or buttermilk
1 teaspoon vanilla	1 cup coarsely chopped hard, green pear
2 cups all-purpose flour	½ cup chopped pecans
½ teaspoon salt	

Preheat oven to 350°. Cream butter and sugar; gradually add in eggs one at a time. Add vanilla. Combine flour, salt, baking powder and nutmeg; add to egg mixture; add yogurt or buttermilk; stir in pears and pecans. Pour into buttered loaf pan. Bake 1 hour.

DAIRY   *Phyllis Kasover*

Arlene's Pumpkin Bread

1 cup oil	1 teaspoon baking powder
3 cups sugar	1 teaspoon nutmeg
4 eggs, beaten	1 teaspoon allspice
1 (15 ounce) can pumpkin	1 teaspoon cinnamon
3½ cups flour	½ teaspoon cloves
2 teaspoons salt	⅔ cup water
2 teaspoons baking soda	

Preheat oven to 350°. Cream oil and sugar. Add eggs and pumpkin. Mix well. Sift flour, salt, baking soda, baking powder, nutmeg, allspice, cinnamon and cloves. Add to pumpkin mixture, alternating with water. Pour into 2 greased and floured loaf pans. Bake 1½ hours. Cool 15 minutes in pan then cool on wire rack.

Makes 2 loaves

PARVE   *Arlene Kleinberg Goldstein*

Pumpkin Bread

1½ cups sugar

½ cup canola oil

2 eggs

1 cup canned pumpkin

1¾ cups flour

¼ teaspoon baking powder

1 teaspoon baking soda

1 teaspoon salt

½ teaspoon cloves

½ teaspoon cinnamon

½ teaspoon nutmeg

½ teaspoon allspice

⅓ cup water

½ cup raisins, optional

½ cup chopped nuts, optional

Preheat oven to 350°. Mix sugar, oil, eggs, pumpkin, flour, baking powder, baking soda, salt, cloves, cinnamon, nutmeg, allspice and water together. Stir in raisins and nuts, if using. Bake 1 hour or until toothpick comes out clean.

You can double recipe for the 1 pound can of pumpkin.

This was my Aunt Anne's specialty. She would bring it from Chicago to the beach every summer. It is delicious for breakfast with coffee or for dessert with dinner! A great Thanksgiving treat, also!

PARVE   *Esther B. Labovitz*

Strawberry Nut Bread

3	cups all-purpose flour	3	eggs, beaten
1	teaspoon baking soda	1	cup vegetable oil
1/2	teaspoon salt	2	(10 ounce) packages frozen, sliced strawberries, thawed
1	tablespoon ground cinnamon		
2	cups sugar	1	cup pecan pieces

Preheat oven to 350°. Combine flour, baking soda, salt, cinnamon and sugar. Mix well. Combine eggs, oil and strawberries. Add to flour mixture; mix well. Pour batter into 2 greased and floured 9x5x3 loaf pans. Bake 1 hour or until toothpick inserted in center of loaf comes out clean.

Makes 2 loaves

Easy to freeze. Makes great gifts.

PARVE   Kathie Cohen

Zucchini Muffins

3	cups raw, chopped zucchini	1/4	teaspoon salt
1/2	cup chopped onion	1/4	teaspoon pepper
4	eggs	1	teaspoon parsley
1/2	cup oil	1/2	teaspoon oregano
1	cup Bisquick	1/2	cup Parmesan cheese

Preheat oven to 350°. Mix zucchini, onion, eggs, oil, Bisquick, salt, pepper, parsley, oregano and cheese. Pour into greased muffin tins. Bake 30-40 minutes or until lightly browned.

Easy to make and freezes well.

DAIRY   Marion Varon

Pumpkin Muffins

2½ cups sugar, divided

3 cups + 5 tablespoons all-purpose flour

2½ teaspoons ground cinnamon, divided

4 tablespoons cold butter, cut into pieces

1 teaspoon ground nutmeg

1 teaspoon ground cloves

1 tablespoon + 1 teaspoon pumpkin pie spice

1 teaspoon salt

1 teaspoon baking soda

4 large eggs

2 cups canned pumpkin

1¼ cups vegetable oil

Preheat oven to 350°. Combine ½ cup sugar, 5 tablespoons flour and 1½ teaspoons cinnamon in small bowl; whisk to blend. Add butter pieces; cut into dry ingredients with pastry blender or two forks until mixture is coarse and crumbly. Transfer to refrigerator until ready to use. Line muffin pans with paper liners. Combine 3 cups flour, 1 teaspoon cinnamon, nutmeg, cloves, pumpkin pie spice, salt and baking soda; whisk to blend. In bowl of electric mixer combine eggs, 2 cups sugar, pumpkin and oil. Mix on medium-low speed until blended. With mixer on low speed, add in dry ingredients, mixing just until incorporated. Fill muffin cups ⅔ full. Sprinkle small amount of topping mixture on each muffin. Bake 20-25 minutes. Transfer to wire rack to cool.

Makes 24 muffins

DAIRY   *Dana Handmacher*

Barley Casserole

½ cup butter or margarine

1 cup quick cooking, fine pearl barley

1 medium onion, chopped

½ cup slivered almonds

1 (2 ounce) package dry onion soup mix

2 cups chicken broth

1 (3 ounce) can sliced mushrooms, undrained

1 (5 ounce) can sliced water chestnuts, drained

Preheat oven to 350°. Melt butter. Add barley and onions; sauté until light golden color. Add almonds, soup mix and broth; stir. Add mushrooms and water chestnuts; stir well. Place in baking dish; cover; bake 1 hour. Add more liquid if needed.

Serves 6

MEAT   *Betty Ehrlich & Elaine Kirkpatrick*

Bulgur – Cracked Wheat

1 medium onion, chopped

3 tablespoons oil

2 cups water

2 tablespoons tomato sauce

1 teaspoon salt

1 cup bulgur

1 cup garbanzos, rinsed, optional

Sauté onion in oil; add water, tomato sauce and salt. Bring to boil; add bulgur and garbanzos, if using. Bring back to boil; lower heat; cover; simmer 20 minutes or until bulgur and garbanzos are tender.

PARVE   *Traditional Sephardic Recipe*

Cornbread Dressing

1	tablespoon oil	6	cups chicken or turkey broth
1	cup self-rising cornmeal, not cornmeal mix	1	stalk celery, chopped
¼	cup flour	1	medium onion, chopped
¼	teaspoon salt	¼	cup finely chopped parsley
¼	teaspoon baking powder	1	teaspoon ground sage
¼	teaspoon baking soda	¼	teaspoon black pepper
1	egg, beaten	½	teaspoon salt
1	cup buttermilk	4	cups cornbread crumbs
¼	cup water	2	slices white bread, crumbled

Preheat oven to 450°. For cornbread, put oil in seasoned 10-inch cast iron skillet or 8x8 baking pan. Coat entire surface; place in oven to heat. In medium bowl, stir together cornmeal, flour, salt, baking powder and baking soda. Add egg, milk and water. Mix until moist. Do not over mix. Pour batter into skillet or pan. Bake 15 minutes, or until lightly browned. This part can be prepared ahead of time and frozen up to a month. To assemble dressing, preheat oven to 350°. Crumble room temperature cornbread into bite-size pieces; set aside. In a large boiler, combine broth, celery, onion and parsley; bring to boil. Cook until vegetables are transparent. Add sage, pepper and salt. Add cornbread and white breadcrumbs, mixing until liquid is absorbed. Spoon dressing into greased 3-quart dish. Bake 45 minutes or until lightly browned.

Serves 10 to 12

MEAT   Jo Anne H. Rousso

Cheese Grits

6-6½ cups water
1½ cups grits, cook until water
    almost gone
½ cup butter

1 pound Velveeta cheese, chunked
2 teaspoons salt
3 eggs, beaten
6-7 drops Tabasco

Preheat oven to 300°. Bring water to boil in large pot. Add grits; cook on low heat until water is evaporated. Stir often. Add butter and cheese, stir until melted. Add salt, eggs and Tabasco; stir until well blended. Place in 9x13 baking dish. Grits will be thin. Bake 1 hour.

Great for breakfast or as a side dish for supper. Can be frozen.

DAIRY *Nancy Taylor*

Grits Casserole

4 cups water
1 teaspoon salt
½ teaspoon black pepper
1 teaspoon garlic powder, optional
1 cup quick cooking grits

2 tablespoons butter
1½ cups grated mild Cheddar
    cheese, divided
4 eggs, beaten
½ cup milk

Preheat oven to 350°. In a large saucepan bring water to boil. Add salt, pepper and garlic powder. Gradually stir in grits. Lower heat; simmer 5-7 minutes, stirring occasionally. Remove from heat; stir in butter and 1 cup cheese. In a small bowl mix eggs with milk, add to grits; stir. Pour grits into greased, 2-quart dish. Top with remaining cheese. Bake 1 hour.

DAIRY *Leslie Capp*

Easy Cheese Grits

1	cup quick grits, not instant	1	(10 ounce) block Velveeta cheese, cut in cubes
3½	cups water	¼	teaspoon garlic powder
1	teaspoon salt		
½	cup butter, cut in pieces		

Cook grits with water and salt according to directions on box. Add butter and Velveeta; stir until combined and melted. Add garlic powder; stir. Serve immediately.

DAIRY *Diane K. Blondheim*

Arroz – Pink Sephardic Rice

1	cup long-grain rice	1½	cups water
1	teaspoon salt	2	tablespoons tomato sauce
2	tablespoons oil		

Rinse rice; drain. Combine water, salt, oil and tomato sauce in 2-quart saucepan. Bring to boil. Add rice; bring to boil again. Stir once. Lower heat to simmer; cook 20 minutes or until all liquid evaporates. Use fork to lift rice from bottom of pan to check for doneness. Stir and serve.

Serves 4 to 6

Many cooks substitute meat or chicken broth for some or all of water. It is also common to add ingredients such as cooked garbanzo beans, cooked lentils, onions, mushrooms, chopped fresh tomatoes, or other vegetables. Decrease amount of liquid if using vegetables that have a lot of moisture.

PARVE OR MEAT *Traditional Sephardic Recipe*

B. C. Rice

¼ cup margarine	1 (10.5 ounce) can beef consommé
1 cup uncooked converted rice	
1 (10.5 ounce) can French onion soup	1 (4 ounce) can sliced mushrooms, drained

Preheat oven to 300°. Melt margarine in 8-inch square baking dish. Stir in rice, soup, consommé and mushrooms. Cover; bake 45 minutes or until liquid is absorbed and rice is tender.

Double recipe for 9x13 baking dish.

Serves 4 to 6

B. C. stands for Blake Cohen, my grandson, who named this dish.

DAIRY   *Kathie Cohen*

Pearl's Rice

1 cup rice, divided	2 teaspoons salt
1½ cups water	1 tablespoon oil

Brown ½ cup rice in oven. Bring water to boil; add salt; add oil; add all of rice. Cover; lower heat. Simmer, undisturbed, 20 minutes; fluff with fork. Cook until all water is evaporated and rice is tender.

You may substitute chicken or vegetable bouillon for water; reduce salt to 1 teaspoon.

PARVE OR MEAT   *Pearl C. Hasson*

Marion Fast's Rice Mold

1 cup uncooked rice
1 (1 ounce) envelope dry onion
  soup mix
¼ cup butter or margarine
2 cups boiling water

1 cup frozen peas
1 (7 ounce) can sliced mushrooms
1 (7 ounce) can sliced water
  chestnuts

Preheat oven to 350°. Combine rice, soup mix and butter or margarine
in boiling water. Place in 9x13 dish. Cover; bake 40 minutes. Add peas,
mushrooms and water chestnuts to rice mixture. Continue to bake 20 minutes,
covered.

DAIRY   *Marsha Orange*

Rice & Noodle Casserole

½ cup butter
1 (8 ounce) package fine noodles
2 cups uncooked Minute Rice
1 teaspoon soy sauce
2 (14.5 ounce) cans chicken broth
1 cup water

1 (1 ounce) package onion soup
  mix
½ cup sliced fresh mushrooms,
  optional
½ cup sliced almonds, optional
½ cup sliced water chestnuts,
  optional

Preheat oven to 350°. Melt butter in medium skillet. Add noodles; stir over
medium heat until browned. Mix rice, soy sauce, broth, water, onion soup and
any optional ingredients you choose in greased 2-quart baking dish. Bake 45
minutes.

MEAT   *Sue R. Jaffe*

Rice Pilaf with Orzo & Mushrooms

¼ cup butter, divided	Pinch pepper
1 onion, diced	1 cup vegetable broth
¼ cup fresh parsley, minced	4 cups water
2 small cloves garlic, minced	½ cup orzo pasta, uncooked
½ cup white rice	¾ pound mushrooms, sliced
½ teaspoon dried basil	½ cup dry vermouth
Pinch salt	

Melt 1½ tablespoons butter in a medium saucepan with a tight fitting lid, over medium heat. Add onions, parsley and ½ of minced garlic. Cook until onions are softened, about 5 minutes. Add rice, basil, salt and pepper. Stir well to coat rice with butter. Add broth; bring to a boil; stir well. Reduce heat to low; cover; cook undisturbed 20 minutes. Remove from heat; let stand, undisturbed, 10 minutes. Meanwhile, bring water to a boil. Add pinch of salt and orzo. Cook 8 minutes or until tender. Drain; toss with ½ tablespoon butter. Set aside. Melt remaining 2 tablespoons butter in a large skillet over medium-high heat. Sauté remaining garlic 1 minute or less. Do not let garlic brown. Add mushrooms; sauté until mushrooms are browned and all of liquid has evaporated. Season with salt and pepper; add vermouth. Cook 3 minutes; remove from heat. When rice is done, place in a large bowl. Add orzo and mushrooms. Gently toss. Serve while hot.

Serves 4

DAIRY *Nick G. Ashner*

Fideo – Vermicelli

1 (8 ounce) package vermicelli	2 tablespoons oil
2 cups water	1 teaspoon salt
2 tablespoons tomato sauce	

Spread vermicelli on baking sheet; brown in 350° oven until golden. Watch carefully; it browns fast. Bring water, tomato sauce, oil and salt to boil. Add vermicelli; stir; lower heat; cover; simmer undisturbed 15 minutes. Toss with fork; recover; cook until all water has evaporated. More water may be added if noodles are not done. Remove from heat; sprinkle a few drops of water over noodles; stir. Leave lid off; allow steam to escape. Serve immediately.

May substitute chicken or vegetable broth for water.

PARVE OR MEAT *Traditional Sephardic Recipe*

Artichokes & Celery

1 chicken bouillon cube
1/4 cup water
1 tablespoon oil
1/2 teaspoon salt
1 tablespoon lemon juice

1/2 teaspoon sugar
2 stalks celery
2-3 carrots, optional
1 (14 ounce) can whole artichoke hearts

In medium saucepan, mix bouillon cube, water, oil, salt, lemon juice and sugar. Cut celery and carrots if using, into 2-inch pieces. Add to liquid. Cover; cook until vegetables are tender crisp. Add artichokes; simmer 10 minutes.

PARVE   Jeanette C. Rousso

Marinated Asparagus

1 pound fresh asparagus
1/4 cup chopped pecans
1/4 cup soy sauce

1/4 cup cider vinegar
1/4 cup sugar
2 tablespoons oil

Steam asparagus until tender crisp, about 10 minutes. Immediately plunge into ice water for 10 minutes; drain. Place in dish no more than 2 inches high; sprinkle pecans on top. Mix soy sauce, vinegar, sugar and oil. Pour over asparagus and nuts. Marinate at least 2 hours, no longer than 24 hours. Serve chilled.

Serves 6 to 8

PARVE   Mae Cohen

Fiery Chipotle Baked Beans

4   ounces spicy kosher sausage, thinly sliced
2¹/₂ cups chopped onion
1   cup chicken broth
¹/₃ cup packed brown sugar
¹/₃ cup cider vinegar
¹/₃ cup bottled chili sauce
¹/₃ cup dark molasses or maple syrup
2   teaspoons dry mustard

2   teaspoons chipotle-chili powder
¹/₂ teaspoon salt
¹/₄ teaspoon ground cloves
¹/₄ teaspoon allspice
1   (15 ounce) can black beans, rinsed, drained
1   (15 ounce) can kidney beans, rinsed, drained
1   (15 ounce) can pinto beans, rinsed, drained

Preheat oven to 325°. Cook sausage 2 minutes in Dutch oven, medium high heat. Add onion; sauté 5 minutes, stirring occasionally. Stir in broth, brown sugar, vinegar, chili sauce, syrup, mustard, chili powder, salt, cloves, all spice and beans. Bake uncovered 1 hour.

Freezes well.

Serves 10

MEAT   *Samye Kermish*

Fasulia – Pole Beans

2   pounds fresh pole beans
2   teaspoons vegetable oil
1   teaspoon salt
2   medium tomatoes, peeled, chopped

1   cup water
1   onion, chopped
¹/₂ teaspoon sugar
1   teaspoon lemon juice, optional

String beans, cut off tips and cut into halves; rinse; place in saucepan. Add oil, salt, tomatoes, water, onion, sugar and lemon juice, if using. Cover; cook on low heat until tender, 30 minutes-1 hour.

May substitute 1 cup canned tomatoes or ¹/₂ cup tomato sauce for fresh tomatoes. May leave onion whole. May add ¹/₂ pound sautéed beef short ribs or beef stew meat.

Serves 6 to 8

PARVE OR MEAT   *Traditional Sephardic Recipe*

Carrot Soufflé

1	pound carrots	3	tablespoons flour
½	cup butter	1	teaspoon baking powder
3	eggs	1	teaspoon vanilla
¾	cup sugar		

Preheat oven to 350°. Cook carrots until tender; drain; pour into food processor. Add butter, eggs, sugar, flour, baking powder and vanilla. Purée until smooth. Pour into 8-cup soufflé dish. Bake 45 minutes. Serve immediately.

Serves 6 to 8

DAIRY   *Samye Kermish*

Apio Con Avas – Celery & Great Northern Beans

1	(16 ounce) can great Northern beans	¼	teaspoon sugar
5	ribs celery, cut in 2-inch pieces	2	tablespoons vegetable oil
2	tablespoons tomato sauce, optional		Pepper to taste
1	cup chicken broth or 1 chicken bouillon cube dissolved in 1 cup hot water		Juice of ½ lemon

Rinse beans thoroughly in cold water; drain; set aside. Put celery, tomato sauce, if using, chicken broth, sugar, oil, pepper and lemon juice in saucepan. Cook at just below boiling until celery is tender crisp, about 10 minutes. Add more water during cooking as necessary. Pour beans over celery; turn off burner. When ready to serve, heat to just below boiling.

If you have left over roast or chicken, cut into chunks; add when you add beans. Either way it's good served with Arroz – pink Sephardic rice.

Serves 3

MEAT   *Corinne F. Capilouto*

Carnabeet – Cauliflower

1	fresh cauliflower	1/2	cup flour, seasoned with salt
3	ribs celery, chopped	1	egg, beaten
3	tablespoons tomato sauce		Juice of 1 lemon
1	medium potato, cut up, optional		Vegetable oil
1	chopped onion, optional		Salt to taste

Preheat oven to 350°. Rinse cauliflower; take out core, leaving cauliflower in one piece. Place in boiling, salted water 5 minutes. Drain well; cut into flowerets; set aside. Cook celery, tomato sauce, potato and onion, if using, in water 15 minutes. Dip tops of cauliflower in flour, then in egg; brown in oil; drain on paper towels. Line bottom of 3-quart dish with potatoes and celery pieces, reserving liquid. Add cauliflower; pour reserved liquid over cauliflower; squeeze lemon juice over all. Cover; bake 20 minutes. Uncover; bake 30 minutes or until liquid is almost all evaporated and cauliflower is golden brown.

Serves 12 to 16

PARVE *Sephardic Dinner 2007*

Celery Casserole

4	cups sliced celery, 1-inch pieces	1	(15 ounce) can cream of mushroom soup
1/4	cup diced pimento		
1	(5 ounce) can sliced water chestnuts, drained	1/4	cup soft breadcrumbs
		1/4	cup slivered almonds, toasted
		2	tablespoons melted butter

Preheat oven to 350°. Cook celery in small amount boiling water, about 8 minutes; drain. Mix celery, pimento, water chestnuts and soup. Turn into buttered casserole dish. Top with breadcrumbs, almonds and melted butter. Bake 35-40 minutes or until brown and bubbly.

Serves 6

DAIRY *Betty Ehrlich*

Corn Pudding

½ cup margarine

2 eggs

1 box corn muffin mix

1 cup light sour cream

1 (14.75 ounce) can cream corn

1 (15.25 ounce) can whole kernel corn, undrained

Preheat oven to 350°. Melt margarine in microwave; set aside. Beat eggs in large bowl. Add corn muffin mix, sour cream, cream corn and undrained whole kernel corn. Mix well; add melted margarine. Spray 9x13 baking pan or 2-quart dish with cooking spray. Bake 50 minutes or until center is set and golden brown.

Serves 8 to 10

Every Thanksgiving I make a double recipe to take to the Capouano's lake house. Aunt Sylvia requests this every year and I am not allowed to bring anything other than my corn pudding. It has been a big hit for years.

DAIRY

Esther C. Miller

Corn Soufflé

½ cup butter

½ cup sugar

1 tablespoon flour

½ cup half-and-half

2 eggs, beaten

1½ teaspoons baking powder

2 (11 ounce) cans Green Giant Crisp Super Sweet Yellow and White whole kernel corn, undrained

Preheat oven to 350°. Spray 2-quart deep baking dish with cooking spray. Heat butter and sugar in small saucepan. Stir in flour. Remove from heat. Add milk, eggs and baking powder. Fold in corn. Pour into baking dish. Place dish in pan with 1 inch hot water. Bake 1 hour or until set in middle.

Serves 6

DAIRY

Diane Blondheim

Shoepeg Corn Casserole

2   (16 ounce) cans shoepeg corn, drained
1   (16 ounce) can French style green beans, drained
½   teaspoon pepper
1   (14.5 ounce) can cream of celery soup
1   (8 ounce) carton sour cream
1   small onion, sautéed
1   cup grated mild Cheddar cheese
1   tube Ritz crackers, crushed
½   cup butter

Preheat oven to 350°. Mix corn, green beans, pepper, soup, sour cream, onion and cheese. Pour into 13x9 lightly buttered baking dish. Top with crackers. Melt butter; drizzle on top. Bake 30 minutes or until hot.

Sometimes I use two cans of green beans.

Serves 12 to 16

DAIRY   Elaine Kirkpatrick

Eggplant Sandwiches

Fresh eggplant
Oil for sautéing
Italian seasoning, to taste
Swiss cheese
Fresh tomatoes, sliced

Slice eggplant into ½-inch circles. Sauté in olive oil; sprinkle with Italian seasoning. Stack 1 slice eggplant, 1 slice Swiss cheese, 1 slice tomato and 1 slice eggplant. Wrap in foil. Repeat for each serving. Grill 5 minutes or until eggplant is soft and cheese is melted.

DAIRY   Wendy Finkelstein

Ratatouille

1	medium yellow onion, chopped	2	tablespoons dried basil
3	cloves garlic, chopped	2	tablespoons dried parsley
1	stalk celery, sliced	2	bay leaves
2	tablespoons olive oil	3-4	whole allspice
1	medium eggplant	1	teaspoon kosher salt
1	green bell pepper	¼	teaspoon pepper
1	red or yellow bell pepper	¼	cup red wine
1	(16 ounce) can diced tomatoes	2	small zucchinis, sliced
1	teaspoon Worcestershire sauce		

Sauté onion, garlic and celery in olive oil until soft and yellow; do not brown; set aside. Peel eggplant; cut into approximately 2-inch squares; set aside. Seed and cut peppers into about 2-inch squares; set aside. Pour tomatoes into soup pot; add onion and garlic. Fill tomato can with water; add to pot. Bring to boil. Reduce heat to simmer. Add eggplant and peppers. Add Worcestershire sauce, basil, parsley, bay leaves, all spice, salt and pepper. Maintain heat at simmer. Add wine; bring back to boil. Reduce heat to simmer; cook covered until eggplant is fork tender. Add zucchini; cook 20 minutes. Serve over rice.

PARVE   *Marian Shinbaum*

Bamia – Baked Okra

1 pound fresh okra, tender young pods or whole frozen

1 cup water for fresh okra, ½ cup for frozen

1 clove minced garlic or ½ teaspoon garlic salt

1 fresh tomato or 2 tablespoons tomato sauce

Juice of 1 lemon

2 tablespoons oil

½ teaspoon salt

Preheat oven to 350°. Wash fresh okra; cut off tips. Cut around stem end to form a cone; do not cut into pod. If using frozen, partially separate pods. Bring water to boil; add garlic, tomato or tomato sauce, lemon juice, oil and salt. Add okra. Cover; simmer 20 minutes. Transfer to baking dish; bake uncovered 30-40 minutes or until lightly brown and liquid has evaporated.

PARVE   *Traditional Sephardic Recipe*

Okra, Corn and Tomatoes by Harold Ehrlich

2½ cups fresh sliced okra cut into ½-inch slices or 2 (10 ounce) packages frozen cut okra

Vegetable oil for browning

1½ cups fresh corn kernels or 1 (10 ounce) package frozen whole kernel corn

2 (14 ounce) cans diced tomatoes, undrained

1 (6 ounce) can tomato paste

Salt to taste

Pepper to taste

Your favorite seasoned salt to taste

Garlic powder to taste

Onion powder to taste

Hot sauce to taste

In large frying pan, lightly brown okra in small amount of oil; drain. Add corn, tomatoes and tomato paste. Season as desired with salt, pepper, seasoned salt, garlic powder, onion powder and hot sauce. Simmer slowly until vegetables are tender, liquid is reduced and mixture is fairly thick. Add water if needed.

Can be frozen.

PARVE   *Betty Ehrlich & Elaine Kirkpatrick*

Fried Okra

1 pound fresh okra	2 cups cornmeal, not cornmeal mix or cornbread mix
2 teaspoons salt	Vegetable oil for frying

Wash okra; pat dry; cut off tips and stem ends. Cut pods into ¼-inch slices. Sprinkle with salt; toss to distribute salt. Lay slices in single layer on paper towels. Cover with paper towels; rest 10 minutes. Place cornmeal in zip-top plastic bag. Add okra; seal; shake to coat. Pour into dry colander; shake off excess cornmeal. Pour about ⅛-inch vegetable oil in 10-12-inch seasoned cast iron skillet, or any thick skillet. Heat skillet until test okra slice sizzles. Add single layer of okra. Don't overfill skillet; pieces should not touch each other after they begin to cook. Watch skillet carefully; maintain medium high heat; stir often. Cook until just golden brown, 3-5 minutes. Remove with slotted spoon; transfer to paper towel lined pan. Continue frying process; layer each batch on paper towels in pan. Serve immediately.

To re-warm, put okra in single layer on ungreased baking pan; warm in preheated 400° oven about 5 minutes.

Serves 4, if people take normal size portions.

My parents, Cleve and Elizabeth Howington had an okra partnership...he grew it, she cooked it. She prepared it several ways but fried was our favorite. What a disappointment when I grew up and found out frozen from the grocery store okra hardly resembled Mama's. Most commercially prepared fried okra is battered. Mama's was simply tossed in corn meal, making it lighter. Even though I make it like Mama did, mine is never quite as good as hers. Nobody cooks like Mama!

PARVE   Jo Anne H. Rousso

Onion Pie

1 cup Ritz cracker crumbs	³/₄ cup milk
¹/₄ cup margarine	Salt to taste
2 tablespoons butter	Pepper to taste
6 cups chopped Vidalia onions	¹/₂ cup grated Cheddar cheese
2 eggs	

Preheat oven to 350°. Crush crackers to make crumbs; mix with margarine; press into 8-inch pie plate. Sauté onions in butter. Spoon onions into crust. Beat eggs, milk, salt and pepper. Pour over onions. Sprinkle cheese. Bake 30 minutes.

If Vidalia onions not available add 2 tablespoons sugar to mix.

DAIRY   *Nomie Sharker*

Scalloped Potatoes

6 tablespoons margarine	3¹/₂ cups chicken stock
¹/₂ cup flour	9-10 large Idaho potatoes, peeled, sliced into ¹/₄-inch slices
2 large onions, chopped	Freshly ground black pepper
¹/₂ cup mayonnaise	Paprika
¹/₂ teaspoon salt	

Preheat oven to 350°. Spray 9x13 glass or ceramic baking pan with cooking spray. In a large pot, melt margarine over medium-high heat; add flour, stirring constantly. Add onions, mayonnaise, salt and chicken stock; stir until smooth. Cook until sauce thickens. Place ¹/₃ of sauce in bottom of pan. Layer ¹/₂ of potatoes, overlapping slices. Repeat layers, ending with sauce. Sprinkle pepper and paprika. Bake uncovered 1¹/₂ hours or until golden.

Serves 10 to 12

MEAT   *Marie Berlin*

Maw Maw's Sweet Potato Casserole

3	cups cooked, mashed, sweet potatoes	1	teaspoon vanilla
3/4	cup sugar	1/3	cup milk
1	cup cold unsalted butter, cut into 1/2-inch cubes, divided	1/2	cup flour
		1	cup brown sugar
2	eggs, beaten	1	cup chopped nuts, optional
			Miniature marshmallows, optional

Preheat oven to 350°. Combine potatoes, sugar, 1/2 cup butter, eggs, vanilla and milk in large bowl. Mix with electric mixer until well blended. Pour into greased 9x13 baking dish. For topping mix, stir together flour and brown sugar; cut in remaining 1/2 cup butter with a pastry blender. Mixture should hold together when squeezed, but crumble apart easily. Stir in pecans. Cover top of casserole with topping mix or miniature marshmallows. Bake 25 minutes.

Serves 12 to 16

DAIRY   *Jo Anne H. Rousso*

Sweet Potatoes

2	(18 ounce) cans sweet potatoes	2	tablespoons water
1/2	cup apple butter	1/2	teaspoon ground cinnamon
1/4	cup brown sugar, packed	2	tablespoons margarine

Preheat oven to 325°. Pour sweet potatoes into 9x13 baking dish. Mix apple butter, brown sugar, water and cinnamon. Spoon mixture over potatoes. Dot with margarine. Bake 30 minutes covered with foil. Remove foil; bake for 10 minutes.

DAIRY   *Linda Taffet*

Spinaca con Garbanzos – Spinach and Chick Peas

1   pound fresh leaf spinach or
      1 (10 ounce) package frozen
      leaf spinach
2   tablespoons oil
1   onion, chopped
2   tablespoons tomato sauce

1   teaspoon salt
    Juice of ½ lemon
½   cup water or chicken broth
1   (15 ounce) can garbanzo beans,
      rinsed, drained

Wash and dry fresh spinach, cut into small pieces, leaving stems. Or, cut semi frozen spinach into small squares; set aside. Sauté onion in oil; drain. Add spinach, tomato sauce, salt, lemon juice and water or chicken broth. Cook 10 minutes covered. Lower heat; add beans; simmer uncovered 10 minutes.

PARVE OR MEAT   *Sephardic Dinner 2007*

Spinach Artichoke Casserole

1   small onion, chopped
¼   cup butter
1   (8 ounce) package cream cheese
3   packages frozen chopped
      spinach, drained, squeezed

    Dash salt
1   tablespoon lemon juice
1   (14 ounce) can quartered
      artichokes, drained
    Breadcrumbs, optional

Preheat oven to 350°. Sauté onion in butter until clear; do not brown. Lower heat; add cream cheese; blend until melted; remove from heat. Add spinach, salt and lemon juice; stir until blended. Place artichokes in 9x13 glass baking pan sprayed with cooking spray. Top with spinach mixture. Top with breadcrumbs if using. Bake 30 minutes.

Serves 12 to 16

DAIRY   *Sylvia Capouano*

Calavasa – Squash

1	pound small yellow squash	1	tablespoon parsley, optional
1	tablespoon oil	½	cup water
2	tablespoons tomato sauce or 1 fresh tomato, chopped	1	chicken bouillon cube
1	clove garlic, minced and/or 1 medium onion, chopped		Salt to taste

Preheat oven to 350°. Peel, wash and cut squash lengthwise into halves and/or quarters depending on the size of squashes. Place in shallow pan. In a small saucepan, mix oil, tomato sauce, garlic and/or onion, parsley if using, water, bouillon cube and salt. Simmer 5 minutes. Pour over squash; bake, uncovered 30 minutes or until liquid is almost evaporated.

Serves 4 to 6

MEAT *Sephardic Dinner 2007*

Roasted Vegetables

1	small butternut squash, cubed	2	tablespoons chopped fresh rosemary
2	red bell peppers, seeded, diced	4	tablespoons olive oil
1	sweet potato, peeled, cubed	2	tablespoons balsamic vinegar
3	Yukon Gold potatoes, cubed		Salt to taste
1	red onion, quartered		Freshly ground black pepper
1	tablespoon chopped fresh thyme		

Preheat oven to 475°. In large bowl, combine squash, bell peppers and potatoes. Separate onion quarters into pieces; add to mixture. In small bowl, stir together thyme, rosemary, olive oil, vinegar, salt and pepper. Toss with vegetables until coated. Spread evenly on large roasting pan. Roast 35-40 minutes or until vegetables are cooked through and browned, stirring every 10 minutes.

Serves 12

PARVE *Rebbetzin Irene E. Kramer*

Roslyn's Squash Casserole

4-5 pounds yellow squash
1 cup onion, chopped
1 cup butter
4 eggs
3 cups fine cracker crumbs

1 teaspoon Worcestershire sauce
1 teaspoon mayonnaise
Salt to taste
Pepper to taste
Paprika

Preheat oven to 350°. Boil squash in salted water; drain and mash; set aside. Sauté onion in butter; set aside. In large bowl, beat eggs well; mix in cracker crumbs. Add squash, onions, Worcestershire sauce, mayonnaise, salt and pepper. Pour mixture into greased 9x13 baking dish. Sprinkle paprika on top; bake 1 hour.

Serves 12 to 16

My mother-in-law served this casserole at all of our family holidays and the tradition continues today. For years her three sons didn't know they were eating squash!

DAIRY
Rhonda Blitz

Tomato and Artichoke Casserole

2 tablespoons finely chopped shallots

½ cup finely chopped onion

3 tablespoons butter or margarine

1 (28 ounce) can whole Roma tomatoes

1 (14 ounce) can quartered artichoke hearts in water, drained

½ teaspoon basil

2 tablespoons sugar

Salt to taste

Pepper to taste

Cracker crumbs

Preheat oven to 325°. Sauté shallots and onions in butter or margarine. Drain tomatoes, reserving liquid. Add tomato juice to onions. Quarter tomatoes; add to onions. Add artichoke hearts, basil, sugar, salt and pepper. Place in glass baking dish. Cover with cracker crumbs. Heat until hot, 20-30 minutes.

This is colorful, easy to make, non-starchy, and goes well with beef or poultry.

DAIRY OR PARVE   *Dale B. Evans*

Tomato Pie

1 (9-inch) pie crust

3-4 Roma tomatoes, sliced

3 scallions, sliced

1 teaspoon dried basil

Salt to taste

Pepper to taste

1 cup grated mozzarella cheese

1 cup grated Cheddar cheese

1 cup mayonnaise

Preheat oven to 350°. Cook pie crust 10 minutes to brown. When cool, put tomatoes, scallions and basil on crust. Salt and pepper to taste. Mix cheeses with mayonnaise; spread on top. Bake 30 minutes or until bubbles.

DAIRY   *Sandi Stern*

Zucchini Asian

6   large zucchini squash

1   teaspoon salt

2   tablespoons sesame oil

½   large onion cut into wedges, chunks, or slices

½   cup chopped red bell pepper

1   large clove garlic, diced

¼   cup sesame seeds

¼   cup reduced sodium chicken broth

¼   cup low sodium soy sauce

¼   teaspoon granulated sweetener

½   teaspoon ginger

⅛   teaspoon red pepper flakes, more to taste

Preheat oven to 475°. Slice zucchini in half lengthwise; cut crosswise into 1-inch pieces. Arrange in single layer on baking sheet sprayed with cooking spray. Bake 15 minutes, turning once. Sauté onions in sesame oil until soft; add bell pepper, garlic and sesame seeds; sauté until onions just begin to brown. Add broth, soy sauce, sweetener, ginger and pepper flakes. Reduce heat to medium; cook until ½ of liquid has cooked away. Pour over baked zucchini; toss. Serve immediately.

Serves 10

MEAT   *Jo Anne H. Rousso*

Finishes...

Desserts & Candy
Cakes & Cookies
Pies & Puddings

The finish to every fabulous menu is an elegant show-stopping dessert. Our selection of irresistible goodies will delight both the palate and the eye. Browse through this collection of *"old country"* and modern American favorites. Then go ahead and make your choice — it's sure to be a hit!

Gaby's Baked Apples

12	Granny Smith apples	½	cup margarine
1	can crescent rolls	1	(12 ounce) can evaporated milk
	Cinnamon, to taste	1	cup sugar

Preheat oven to 350°. Peel, core and cut 1 apple into quarters. Wrap a dinner roll around apple quarters; place on buttered baking pan, folded edges down. Repeat with each apple. Sprinkle with cinnamon. Melt margarine, milk and sugar. Pour over apples. Bake 20-30 minutes.

DAIRY   *Gaby Capp*

Baklava – Honey and Nut Pastry

5	cups almonds and/or pecans, chopped fine	½	teaspoon ground cloves, optional
½	cup toasted sesame seed, optional	1	pound phyllo dough
2½	cups sugar, divided	1	cup oil
1	teaspoon cinnamon	1½	cups honey
		1½	cups sugar
		1	cup water

Preheat oven to 350°. Finely chop or grind nuts and sesame seeds, if using. Add 1 cup sugar, cinnamon and cloves, if using; mix well. Divide into 4 equal portions; set aside. Oil 9x13 pan. Place 1 piece phyllo to fit pan; brush with a little oil; repeat to make 4 layers. Keep remaining phyllo covered with damp cloth to keep it moist. Sprinkle one portion of nut filling on 4th layer. Add 2 more layers of phyllo, brushing with oil between layers. Sprinkle 1 portion of nut filling over second layer. Repeat the 4-layer, 2-layer pattern, finishing with 4 layers of phyllo on top. Cut into 1½-inch squares, cutting through to bottom. Bake 5 minutes; reduce heat to 275°; bake 1 hour or until brown. While baklava is cooking prepare syrup. Combine 1½ cups sugar, honey and water. Bring to boil until sticky; do not overcook. It will thicken as it cools. Pour cooled syrup over hot baklava. Freezes well.

PARVE   *Sephardic Dinner 2007*

Berries in a Cloud

3 egg whites
1½ teaspoons vanilla, divided
¼ teaspoon cream of tartar
1 cup sugar
½ cup finely chopped toasted almonds
1 (3 ounce) package cream cheese, softened
½ cup packed brown sugar

½ cup unsweetened cocoa powder
1 tablespoon milk
1 cup whipping cream
Whole strawberries, stems removed
2 squares semisweet chocolate, cut up
2 teaspoons shortening

Preheat oven to 300°. Rest egg whites at room temperature 30 minutes. Cover a baking sheet with parchment paper; draw 9-inch circle on paper; set aside. In large bowl, combine egg whites, 1 teaspoon vanilla and cream of tartar. Beat with mixer at medium speed until soft peaks form, barely holding a shape. Gradually add sugar, 1 tablespoon at a time, beating on high until very stiff peaks form and sugar is almost dissolved. Fold in chopped almonds; spread over circle on baking sheet; build up sides to make nest. Bake 45 minutes. Turn oven off; leave in oven 1 hour. Remove from oven. Lift meringue; peel off paper. Put on serving platter or in air-tight container; cover tightly. In small mixing bowl, beat cream cheese and brown sugar until smooth. Add cocoa powder, milk and ½ teaspoon vanilla; beat until smooth. In another small bowl, beat whipping cream on medium speed until soft peaks form; fold into cocoa mixture. Spoon into meringue shell; top with strawberries, stem side down. Melt chocolate with shortening in saucepan; drizzle over strawberries.

DAIRY   *Pearl C. Hasson*

Adults Ice Cream Sandwich Dessert

16 ice cream sandwiches
1   (16 ounce) container Cool
    Whip, thawed

¹/₄ cup amaretto
1   cup sliced almonds, toasted

Lay 8 ice cream sandwiches in ungreased 9x13 Pyrex pan. Gently press sandwiches causing a little ice cream to bulge out. Stir amaretto into thawed Cool Whip. Spread half Cool Whip mix evenly over sandwiches. Cover with remaining sandwiches. Spread remaining Cool Whip. Top with almonds. Cover and freeze. To serve, remove about 15 minutes before cutting.

Serves 16

DAIRY   *Dale B. Evans*

Cheesecake

3   (8 ounce) packages cream
    cheese
1   cup sour cream
5   eggs, separated
1¹/₄ cups sugar, divided
1   teaspoon vanilla

2   tablespoons cornstarch
1   cup milk
1   teaspoon cream of tartar
1¹/₂ cups graham cracker crumbs
¹/₄ cup butter, melted
1   teaspoon cinnamon

Preheat oven to 350°. Blend cream cheese with sour cream. Add egg yolks; blend. Add 1 cup sugar and vanilla. Mix cornstarch with milk; add to cheese mixture; set aside. Beat egg whites with cream of tartar until stiff peaks form; fold into cheese mixture; set aside. To make crust, combine graham cracker crumbs, butter, ¹/₄ cup sugar and cinnamon; mix well. Pat into bottom of 9 or 10-inch springform pan coming up ¹/₂ the sides. Pour cheese mixture into crust. Bake 1 hour. Turn oven off; leave cake in oven 1 hour.

DAIRY   *Pearl C. Hasson*

Jelly-Roll with Lemon Curd Filling

LEMON CURD

3 large eggs

$1/3$ cup sugar

Grated zest of 1 lemon

$1/2$ cup fresh lemon juice

6 tablespoons unsalted butter, cut into small pieces

$1/2$ teaspoon vanilla extract

Whisk 3 eggs, $1/3$ cup sugar and lemon zest in medium stainless steel or enamel saucepan until light in color. Add lemon juice and butter. Cook over medium heat, whisking constantly until mixture thickens; simmer gently a few seconds. Using a spatula, scrape mixture into medium mesh strainer set over a bowl. Strain filling into bowl; stir in $1/2$ teaspoon vanilla. Let cool; refrigerate to thicken.

JELLY-ROLL

Powdered sugar for rolling jelly-roll and sprinkling

1 cup sifted cake flour

1 teaspoon baking powder

$1/2$ teaspoon salt

3 eggs

1 cup sugar

5 tablespoons cold water

1 teaspoon vanilla extract

Preheat oven to 375°. Line jelly-roll pan with wax paper. Sprinkle a kitchen towel larger than jelly-roll pan with powdered sugar; set aside. Sift flour, baking powder and salt together; set aside. Beat eggs until thick; gradually beat in sugar. Add water and vanilla; beat. Add flour mixture all at one time; beat only until smooth. Pour into pan lined with wax paper; even out batter. Bake 12-15 minutes. Turn onto prepared towel; immediately remove wax paper. Roll jelly-roll while warm; unroll; spread with lemon curd filling; roll back snugly. Thoroughly chill before serving. Just before serving, sprinkle with powdered sugar or frost with fresh whipped cream.

You may substitute any type preserves such as apricot, strawberry, etc. for the lemon curd. This keeps in refrigerator 1 week. For reduced-fat lemon curd, prepare as above decreasing eggs to 2, increase sugar to $3/4$ cup, lemon juice to $2/3$ cup and just 2 tablespoons butter.

DAIRY   *Corinne F. Capilouto*

Cadaiff – Noodle Confection

1	(4 ounce) package very fine noodles	1	cup sugar
2	tablespoons oil	1	cup ground nuts, pecans, walnuts and/or almonds
1³/₄	cups water	¹/₂	teaspoon cinnamon

Preheat oven to 350°. Place noodles in 8x8 Pyrex dish. Sprinkle with oil; toast in oven 7 minutes or until lightly golden. Bring sugar and water to boil; pour over noodles. Bake covered 30 minutes. Mix nuts and cinnamon in bowl. Remove dish from oven; uncover; lightly stir half of nut mixture into noodles. Sprinkle remaining nut mixture over top. Re-cover; bake 10 minutes. When cool, spoon into small paper serving cups.

PARVE   *Sephardic Dinner 2007*

Kadayif

1	pound kataifi pastry dough (thinly shredded phyllo dough)		Few drops water for sprinkling
2	cups ground walnuts or almonds	1	cup sugar
1	teaspoon cinnamon	¹/₂	cup honey
¹/₂	teaspoon ground cloves	¹/₄	cup water
			Juice of ¹/₂ lemon

Preheat oven to 350°. Spread half of dough in well-greased 10-inch pie pan. Mix nuts, cinnamon and cloves. Spread nut mixture over dough; spread rest of dough on top; sprinkle liberally with water. Bake 20 minutes or until top is golden brown. While kadayif is baking, prepare syrup. Combine sugar, honey and water in saucepan. Boil 5 minutes; simmer 15 minutes. Remove from heat; stir in lemon juice. Pour syrup over kadayif. Cool to room temperature before serving.

PARVE   *Gaby Capp*

Ashuplados – Meringues

3   egg whites
1   cup sugar

½   teaspoon vanilla flavoring
½   cup chopped pecans, optional

Preheat oven to 275°. Beat egg whites, adding sugar gradually. Add vanilla. Beat until very stiff. Fold in pecans gently. Drop by teaspoonful on baking sheet lined with wax paper. Bake 30 minutes or until lightly brown.

You may substitute ½ cup chopped dates or ½ cup semisweet chocolate bits for nuts. Suitable for Passover.

Makes 36

PARVE   *Emily Allen*

Frosted Candy Pecans

½   cup sour cream
1½ cups sugar

1½ teaspoons vanilla
3   cups pecan halves

Put sour cream, sugar and vanilla in large saucepan; bring to boil. Cook until drop of mixture forms a soft ball in ice water. Add pecans; toss quickly to coat. Spread in single layer on cookie sheet, separating pieces with a fork. Work quickly; frosting dries fast. Store in air-tight container.

Diane remembers: My father, Dave Kulbersh, used an inertia nut cracker to crack pecans from our front yard as our home was built in a pecan grove. It made the biggest mess and the loudest noise that drove us all crazy. Mom and I would clean up the mess and frost the pecans. Oh how I miss the noise and the mess!

DAIRY   *Diane K. Blondheim & Rita Rosenthal*

Masapan – Marzipan

3 cups whole blanched almonds
1³/₄ cups sugar
2 cups water

Silver drageés (edible silver balls), if desired

Grind almonds as fine as possible. Place sugar and water in double boiler or saucepan with heavy bottom. Bring to boil, removing scum as it forms. Cook until mixture becomes sticky and forms a soft ball in very cold water. Lower heat; gradually add almonds, stirring constantly, until well blended. Continue stirring over low heat 25 minutes or until mixture leaves bottom of pan and has the consistency of soft biscuit dough. Remove from stove; cool completely. Knead until smooth and it is a very soft paste. Divide into 6 equal parts. Roll into strips 1-inch thick and wide. Cut diagonally into diamond shaped pieces ¹/₂ inches long. Decorate with a silver drageés, if using.

Store in tightly sealed jar or freeze. Can be used for Passover.

Masapan is made for very special family occasions, especially celebrations for newborns and weddings. It is usually served with Jordan almonds – white for weddings and mixed pastels for other occasions.

PARVE   *Traditional Sephardic Recipe*

Easy Masapan – Marzipan

2   cups blanched almonds
1   teaspoon lemon juice
1/2 teaspoon pure almond extract

1 1/2 cups powdered sugar
1   large egg white, beaten until frothy

Grind nuts in food processor until fine. Add lemon juice, almond extract and powdered sugar. While processor is running, add egg white slowly, a little at a time. Continue processing until dough rolls up; it will only be a few seconds. Remove from processor; knead thoroughly. Roll into 3 logs, 1-inch thick and wide. Cut into desired size and shape. Freezes well.

Makes approximately 45 pieces

PARVE   *Alice Kleinberg*

Nut Butter Crunch

1   cup butter or 1/2 cup butter and
      1/2 cup margarine
1   cup sugar
2   tablespoons water

1   tablespoon light corn syrup
1/2 cup chocolate chips
2/3 cup finely chopped pecans

In medium saucepan, melt butter on low heat. Add sugar; stir until melted. Add water and syrup. Cook until syrup dropped in cold water becomes brittle, 320°. Don't undercook. Remove from heat; pour onto greased platter or cookie sheet. Mixture should be very thin. Cool until hardened. Melt chocolate over hot water or in microwave. Spread melted chocolate on hardened crunch. Sprinkle nuts on top; pat in. Break into pieces.

DAIRY   *Sylvia Capouano*

Apple Cake – One

2	cups sugar	1/2	cup chopped pecans
1	cup oil	3	cups flour
2	eggs, well beaten	1	teaspoon salt
4	cups peeled diced apples	1	teaspoon soda
1/2	cup raisins, white or dark	3	teaspoons cinnamon

Preheat oven to 350°. Mix sugar, oil and eggs. Add apples, raisins and pecans. Sift flour, salt, soda and cinnamon. Mix by hand into apple mixture. Dough will be very stiff. Bake 1 hour. Test with a toothpick. Bake a little longer if necessary.

PARVE *Clara Berns*

Apple Cake – Two

1 1/2	cups oil	1 1/2	cups chopped pecans
2	cups sugar	3	cups raw apples, peeled, diced
3	large eggs	2	teaspoons vanilla, divided
3	cups flour, sifted with 1 teaspoon salt	1	cup light brown sugar
1	teaspoon baking soda	1/2	cup butter
1	teaspoon baking powder	1/2	cup cream or half-and-half

Preheat oven to 325°. In mixer, combine oil and sugar; add eggs. Sift flour with salt; add to batter. Add baking soda and baking powder. By hand, add pecans, apples and 1 teaspoon vanilla; mix well. Bake in greased 9x13 pan 1 hour. Combine brown sugar, butter, cream and 1 teaspoon vanilla. Cook over medium heat 2 1/2 minutes, stirring constantly; pour over warm cake.

Serves 12 to 15

My mother, Sylvia Rubin, found this recipe in the newspaper in the early 1970's and adapted it to be her own. Since then, it has been a hit in our family.

DAIRY *Barbara Handmacher*

Carrot Cake

³/₄	cup sugar		1¹/₂	cups water
1	cup grated carrot		3	tablespoons oil
1	cup raisins		2	cups flour, white or whole wheat
1	teaspoon cinnamon		2	teaspoons baking soda
1	teaspoon grated nutmeg		¹/₃	teaspoon salt
1	teaspoon ground cloves		1	cup chopped walnuts

Preheat oven to 325°. Grease 9x13 pan with oil. In small saucepan, combine sugar, carrot, raisins, cinnamon, nutmeg, cloves, water and oil. Bring to boil; reduce heat; simmer 5 minutes. Pour into mixing bowl; cool to lukewarm. Add flour, baking soda and salt; mix well. Stir in walnuts. Pour in pan; bake 45 minutes or until cake tester comes out clean.

PARVE *Pauline Witt*

Hot Fudge Sundae Cake

1	cup flour		1	teaspoon vanilla
³/₄	cup sugar		2	cups chopped nuts, divided, optional
2	tablespoons cocoa			
2	teaspoons baking powder		1	cup brown sugar, packed
¹/₄	teaspoon salt		¹/₄	cup cocoa
¹/₂	cup milk		1³/₄	cups boiling water
2	tablespoons vegetable oil			

Preheat oven to 350°. In ungreased 9x9 pan, mix flour, sugar, cocoa, baking powder and salt. Add milk, oil, vanilla and 1 cup nuts, if using; mix with a fork until smooth. Level batter in pan. Sprinkle with brown sugar and cocoa. Pour hot water over batter. Do not stir. Bake 40 minutes. Garnish with 1 cup nuts, if using. Let stand 15 minutes before serving. Spoon vanilla ice cream into dishes; spoon cake on top.

This cake bakes strangely. The cake comes to the top and hot fudge thickens underneath.

Serves 9

DAIRY *Lynne Ginsburg*

Lemon Delight Bundt Cake

2½ cups all-purpose flour

1½ cups sugar

3 teaspoons baking powder

¾ cup orange juice

¾ cup vegetable oil

1½ teaspoons lemon extract

4 large eggs

¾ cup powdered sugar, + more for dusting

⅛ cup lemon juice

Preheat oven to 325°. Grease and flour Bundt pan. Combine flour, sugar and baking powder in large mixing bowl. Add orange juice, oil, lemon extract and eggs. Beat 3-4 minutes at medium speed. Pour into pan. Bake 45-50 minutes or until cake tester comes out clean. Remove cake from oven. Using long thin skewer, poke holes into cake at 1-inch intervals. To make glaze, mix powdered sugar and lemon juice until smooth. Spoon glaze over hot cake, allowing it to run into holes. Allow cake to cool. Remove cake from pan; sprinkle with powdered sugar.

Serves 10 to 12

PARVE   *Marie Berlin*

Pineapple Cake

2 cups flour

2 cups sugar

2 eggs

½ cup oil

1 teaspoon baking soda

1 (20 ounce) can crushed pineapple

8 ounces cream cheese, softened

½ cup margarine, softened

1½ cups powdered sugar

1 teaspoon vanilla extract

1 cup chopped nuts

Preheat oven to 350°. Mix flour, sugar, eggs, oil, baking soda, and pineapple by hand until well blended. Pour into greased 9x13 pan. Bake 20-30 minutes. For icing, mix cream cheese, margarine, powdered sugar and vanilla; stir in nuts. Apply to warm cake.

DAIRY   *Dale B. Evans*

Watergate Cake

1	package white cake mix	$^1/_2$	cup chopped pecans
2	(1.4 ounce) packages pistachio instant pudding mix, divided	$1^1/_4$	cups milk
3	eggs	1	(9 ounce) carton frozen whipped topping
1	cup vegetable oil		Maraschino cherries, optional
1	cup club soda		

Preheat oven to 350°. Mix cake mix, 1 package pudding mix, eggs, oil and club soda; stir in pecans. Bake in greased and floured 13x9 pan 40 minutes. To make frosting, mix remaining pudding mix and milk until thick; fold in whipped topping. Frost cooled cake. Top with cherries if desired.

DAIRY   *Leslie Capp*

Chocolate Chip Pound Cake

1	cup butter or margarine	$^1/_2$	teaspoon salt
$1^1/_2$	teaspoons vanilla	1	cup sour cream
3	eggs	1	(12 ounce) package mini chocolate chips
2	cups sugar		Powdered sugar for dusting
2	teaspoons baking powder		
3	cups all-purpose flour		

Preheat oven to 350°. Cream butter; add vanilla, sugar and eggs; beat until light and fluffy. Add baking powder, flour and salt alternately with sour cream. Blend completely. Add chocolate chips. Pour into greased and floured 10-inch tube pan. Bake 1 hour. Cool at least 2 hours. Dust with powdered sugar.

DAIRY   *Amy Labovitz*

Chocolate Pound Cake

1½	cups butter	½	teaspoon baking powder
3	cups sugar	1	cup milk
3	cups flour	5	eggs
6	tablespoons cocoa	1	teaspoon vanilla

Preheat oven to 350°. Cream butter and sugar until fluffy. Combine flour, cocoa and baking powder. In a small bowl, beat eggs; add milk; stir until incorporated. Alternately add flour mixture and egg mixture to butter and sugar mixture. Add vanilla. Bake 1 hour. Test for doneness; if not ready, give it another 15 minutes.

__DAIRY__   *Nomie Sharker*

Coconut Pound Cake

1	cup butter	1	cup whole milk
½	cup shortening	1	teaspoon vanilla flavoring
3	cups sugar	½	teaspoon rum
5	large eggs	1	(6-8 ounce) package frozen
3	cups flour		coconut
1	teaspoon baking powder		

Preheat oven to 325°. Cream butter, shortening and sugar; add eggs 1 at a time. Add baking powder and flour. Add milk, vanilla, rum and coconut. Spray two 9x5x3 loaf pans with Pam and dust with flour. Pour half batter into each pan. Bake 1½ hours.

__DAIRY__   *Rita Rosenthal*

Sour Cream Pound Cake

1	cup butter	1/2	teaspoon baking soda
3	cups sugar	3	cups sifted flour
6	eggs	1 1/2	teaspoons vanilla
1	cup sour cream		

Preheat oven to 325°. Beat butter and sugar until creamy. Add eggs 1 at a time; beat a little after each. Add baking soda to sour cream. Add sour cream mixture to batter; add flour; add vanilla. Pour into greased and floured Bundt pan. Bake 1 hour and 15 minutes.

DAIRY   *Carol Capouano*

Zucchini Cake

3	eggs	1	teaspoon salt
1 1/2	cups sugar	1	teaspoon baking powder
1	cup oil	1	tablespoon cinnamon
2	cups grated zucchini	2	cups flour
1	tablespoon vanilla	1	cup chopped walnuts or pecans

Preheat oven to 350°. Beat eggs; add sugar, oil, zucchini and vanilla. Sift dry ingredients together; add to mixture. Fold nuts into batter. Pour into two buttered 9x5x3 loaf pans. Bake 1 hour.

PARVE   *Renée Capouano*

French Butter Rum Cake with Pearl Icing

2 cups all-purpose flour	1⅓ cups whole milk, divided
2 teaspoons baking powder	1 teaspoon butter flavor
1½ teaspoons salt, divided	1 teaspoon rum flavor
4 large eggs, room temperature	½ cup shortening
2 cups sugar	1 (16 ounce) box powdered sugar
1 teaspoon vanilla flavor	1 teaspoon almond flavor
½ cup butter	½ teaspoon salt

Preheat oven to 325°. Grease bottom of tube pan, not the sides. Cut wax paper to fit bottom of pan. Grease top of wax paper; sprinkle with a little flour; set aside. Sift flour, baking powder and 1 teaspoon salt together. Sift flour mixture 3 times; set aside. In large bowl, beat eggs; slowly add sugar a little at a time, beating well after each addition; add vanilla; stir; set aside. Melt butter in 1 cup milk. You may want to use double boiler; it is very important that melted butter and milk be lukewarm; it cannot be hot; set aside. Gradually add flour mixture to egg mixture; beat well. Slowly pour in melted butter; mix. Add butter and rum flavorings; mix well. Batter will be thin. Be sure to scrape sides of bowls often while making batter. Pour batter into pan. Bake 45 minutes-1 hour or until toothpick comes out clean. For icing, beat shortening until fluffy; slowly add powdered sugar a little at a time. Gradually add remaining milk, almond flavor and ½ teaspoon salt. Beat until smooth. Cake should be cool before icing.

This cake is delicious with or without the icing and freezes well.

DAIRY   *Ruby Goldfield*

Yard Cake

1½	cups water	1	teaspoon cloves
1½	cups raisins	1	teaspoon nutmeg
¾	cup oil or butter or margarine	1	teaspoon baking soda
1½	cups sugar	½	teaspoon salt
2	eggs	½	cup margarine, softened
3	cups flour	1	box powdered sugar
1	teaspoon cinnamon	¼	cup strong coffee

Preheat oven to 350°. Combine raisins and water. Boil; let sit 20 minutes; drain, reserving liquid. Place raisins on paper towels. Add water to liquid to equal 1 cup; set aside. Cream butter or oil and sugar; add eggs. Sift flour with spices, salt and soda. Add dry mix to creamed mixture, alternating with raisin water; mix well. Pour in greased 11x15 pan. Scatter raisins evenly over batter; press into batter. Bake 30-40 minutes. For frosting, combine margarine, powdered sugar and coffee; beat until creamy. Spread over cooled cake.

Serves 15

When I was young, Mama made this for picnics, family reunions and such, where meals were enjoyed outside, "in the yard". So, I grew up thinking the name came from where we ate the cake. When I asked for the recipe I mentioned that notion and Mama said she always thought it was named such because you could "make it by the yard to feed a lot of people." Who knows! Either explanation works for this easy, old-fashioned recipe.

DAIRY   *Dale B. Evans*

Bourbon Cookies

2	eggs	1/2	teaspoon nutmeg
3/4	cup sugar	1/2	teaspoon cloves
1/2	cup light corn syrup	2	cups flour
1 1/2	teaspoons baking soda	1/4	cup bourbon
1	tablespoon milk or water	4	cups pecan halves, broken in two
1/2	teaspoon cinnamon		

Preheat oven to 350°. Beat eggs; add sugar and syrup. Dissolve baking soda in milk or water; add to batter. Add cinnamon, nutmeg, cloves, flour and bourbon; mix well. Stir in pecan pieces. If batter is too thin, add more flour. Drop by teaspoon onto greased pans. Bake 12-15 minutes or until light brown. Store in an air-tight container.

Make cookies small. Do not overfill teaspoon; they swell.

DAIRY OR PARVE   *Linda Taffet*

Crisp Toffee Bars

1 1/6	cups butter, divided	1	(6 ounce) package semisweet chocolate chips
1 1/2	cups brown sugar, divided	1	cup chopped pecans
1	teaspoon vanilla		
2	cups flour		

Preheat oven to 350°. Cream 1/2 cup butter, 1 cup sugar and vanilla. Add flour. Press mixture into 15x10 jelly-roll pan. Bake 10 minutes. Boil 2/3 cup butter with 1/2 cup brown sugar. Pour over cookie crust; bake 18 minutes. Remove from oven; sprinkle chocolate chips evenly over top. Return to oven 2 minutes. Top with chopped pecans. Cut while warm.

Makes 5 dozen

DAIRY   *Bella Smith*
                                                   Frances Capouya

E-Z Cookies

1   box cake mix, flavor of your choice

½   cup vegetable oil

2   eggs

Chocolate chips, chopped pecans, or if using spice cake mix, add raisins, all optional

Preheat oven to 350°. Combine cake mix, oil, eggs and optional ingredients you choose. Stir with fork until well mixed. Form into small balls; place on parchment lined baking sheet. Bake 8-10 minutes.

My daughter Elyse and her grandmother Zona enjoyed making these when Elyse was a little girl. As you can imagine, this is a perfect recipe for enticing a child into the world of cooking!

DAIRY   *Dale B. Evans*

Brownie-Like Cookies

2   cups sugar

4   eggs

2   teaspoons vanilla

¼   cup shortening

¼   cup butter

4   squares chocolate, melted and cooled

2⅓   cups flour

2   teaspoons baking powder

1   teaspoon salt

½   cup nuts

    Powdered sugar for coating

Preheat oven to 350°. Mix sugar, eggs and vanilla. In a separate bowl, mix shortening, butter and chocolate; add to sugar mixture; mix until blended. Gradually add flour, baking powder and salt, incorporating ingredients after each addition. Fold in nuts. Chill dough 1 hour or more. Shape chilled dough into balls; roll in powdered sugar. Bake 10 minutes.

DAIRY   *Linda Taffet*

Double Dark Decadent Brownies

½ cup + 2 tablespoons light or dark corn syrup, divided	3 eggs
½ cup + 1 tablespoon butter, divided	1 teaspoon vanilla
8 ounces semisweet baking chocolate, divided	1 cup flour
¼ cup sugar	1 cup chopped walnuts
	1 teaspoon milk

Preheat oven to 350°. Grease and flour 9-inch layer cake pan. In large saucepan, bring ½ cup corn syrup and ½ cup butter to boil, stir occasionally. Remove from heat. Add 5 ounces chocolate; stir until melted. Add sugar; stir in eggs one at a time; add vanilla, flour and nuts. Pour into pan. Bake 30 minutes or until toothpick comes out clean. Cool in pan 10 minutes. Remove from pan; cool completely on rack. For glaze, melt 3 ounces baking chocolate with 1 tablespoon butter in small saucepan over low heat; stir often. Remove from heat; stir in 2 tablespoons corn syrup and milk. Pour on top of cake; spread on sides. Let stand 1 hour.

DAIRY *Linda Taffet*

Chocolate Dipped Coconut Macaroons

5⅓ cups sweetened shredded coconut	4 egg whites
⅔ cup sugar	1 teaspoon almond extract
6 tablespoons flour	1 (8-10 ounce) package semisweet chocolate chips, melted
⅛ teaspoon salt	

Preheat oven to 325°. Mix coconut, sugar, flour and salt in large bowl. Add egg whites and almond extract, mixing well. Drop by tablespoonful onto greased and floured baking sheet. Bake 20 minutes or until edges of cookies are golden brown. Remove immediately; place on wire rack to cool. Dip cookies halfway into melted chocolate. Let stand at room temperature or refrigerate on wax paper lined tray 30 minutes or until chocolate is firm.

DAIRY *Frances Capouya*

Golden Bars

²/₃	cup shortening	2	cups brown sugar, firmly packed
1¹/₂	cups sifted all-purpose flour	2	eggs, well beaten
2	teaspoons baking powder	1	teaspoon vanilla
¹/₄	teaspoon salt	³/₄	cup chopped nuts

Preheat oven to 350°. Melt shortening in saucepan; remove from heat. Sift flour, salt and baking powder together. Add melted shortening, brown sugar, beaten eggs and vanilla. Mix until well blended; stir in nuts. Spread in 12x8x1 greased pan. Bake 30-35 minutes. Cool and cut.

Makes 28

PARVE   *Phyllis Kasover*

Scotty's Biscotti

4	cups unbleached flour, or 3 cups unbleached + 1 cup whole wheat	2	cups sugar
		¹/₂	cup canola oil
4	teaspoons baking powder	4	eggs
1	teaspoon salt	2	teaspoons vanilla
		2	cups chopped nuts

Preheat oven to 350°. Combine flour, baking powder and salt; set aside. Beat sugar and oil; add eggs and vanilla. Beat until lemon yellow. Stir in dry ingredients. Stir in chopped nuts. Divide batter into 4 portions. Roll into logs; place on 2 greased cookie sheets. Bake 30 minutes. Remove logs from oven. Slice; place pieces cut side down on cookie sheets. Return to oven; bake 10 minutes until crisp. Cool on wire racks.

Makes about 48

This recipe is from our son Scott. It always amazes me that he learned how to cook on his own! I love that sharing recipes with him is a two-way street!

PARVE   *Toby Gewant*

Lemon Squares

³/₄ cup butter, very cold	2 tablespoons lemon zest
2 cups flour	1 cup lemon juice, fresh squeezed
3¹/₄ cups sugar	Powdered sugar
6 eggs	

Preheat oven to 350°. Line 9x13 pan with foil; spray with oil. Mix butter, 1¹/₂ cups flour and ¹/₄ cup sugar. Mix with fork until coarse crumbs. Press into pan. Bake 20-25 minutes until golden brown. To make filling, mix 3 cups sugar, ¹/₂ cup flour, eggs, lemon zest and juice until well blended. Pour over crust. Bake 35 minutes until edges are golden. Cool in pan; cut into 2x2 bars. Place in individual baking cups; sprinkle with powdered sugar.

DAIRY *Frances Capouya*

Alta Tanta's Mandel Bread

3 cups sifted flour	³/₄ cup oil
¹/₂ teaspoon salt	1 cup sugar
2 tablespoons baking powder	1 teaspoon almond extract
3 large eggs	¹/₂ cup chopped nuts

Preheat oven to 350°. Sift flour, salt, and baking powder together; set aside. Beat eggs, oil, sugar and almond extract. Add dry ingredients and nuts; mix well. On greased cookie sheet, form dough into 4 logs, length of pan. Bake 30 minutes. Cut logs into slices while still warm. Can return slices to oven for 3-5 minutes to dry.

Thanks to my late Aunt Helen's recipe, I got great reviews on the Mandel Bread I made for the Hanukkah Hoopla. Aunt Helen named herself "Alta Tanta" (old aunt in Yiddish)

PARVE *Betty Ziri*

Mandel Bread

4 eggs	Zest of 1 orange or tangerine
1 cup sugar	4 cups flour, divided
Dash of salt	1 tablespoon sugar, optional
1 cup oil	1 tablespoon cinnamon, optional
1 teaspoon vanilla extract	

Preheat oven to 350°. Combine eggs, sugar and salt; beat well. Add oil, vanilla and zest; beat well. Add 3 cups flour, a little at a time; add nuts; stir in remainder of flour. Refrigerate dough 1 hour. Roll dough into 4 logs. If using, mix sugar and cinnamon; sprinkle on logs. Place logs on 2 baking sheets. Bake 20 minutes. Slice logs on bread board; place back on baking pans. Crisp in oven at lowest setting overnight or at 225° for a few hours.

PARVE   *Clara Berns*

Nana's Mandel Bread

3 eggs	Pinch of salt
¾ cup sugar	1 teaspoon vanilla
¾ cup oil	1 teaspoon almond extract
2 cups flour	½ cup chopped pecans
1 teaspoon baking powder	

Preheat oven to 350°. Mix together eggs, sugar and oil. Add flour, baking powder, salt and vanilla. Stir in pecans. Grease shallow loaf pan or 3 metal ice cube trays without separators. Pour batter into pan(s). Bake 30 minutes. Remove; cut into ¼ to ½-inch slices; place on sides in single layer on baking pans. Toast in oven 10 minutes.

You can add cinnamon and sugar to tops before baking or add chocolate chips to batter.

PARVE   *Bonnie London*

Nutty Fingers

1½	cups butter or margarine	4	teaspoons cold water
1½	cups sifted powdered sugar	2	teaspoons vanilla
2	cups finely chopped nuts	5	cups all-purpose flour

Preheat oven to 300°. Mix butter or margarine and powdered sugar. Add nuts; mix. Add water; mix. Add vanilla; mix. Add flour; mix. Roll small portion of dough in shape of a finger. Place on greased cookie sheet; bake until delicate brown. Dust with powdered sugar when removed from cookie sheet.

DAIRY   *Rita Rosenthal*

Travados – Almond and Honey Filled Cookies

4	cups ground almonds	½	teaspoon ground cloves
1	cup sugar, divided	1	cup oil
4	tablespoons honey, not raw, light in color	1	egg
1	cup water, divided	½	teaspoon baking soda
½	teaspoon ground cinnamon	5	cups all-purpose White Lily flour, approximately, sifted

Preheat oven to 350°. Mix almonds, ½ cup sugar, honey, ½ cup water, cinnamon and cloves; set aside. Mix oil, ½ cup sugar, ½ cup water and egg; set aside. Sift baking soda and flour. Add flour to oil. Add more flour mix as needed to form medium dough. Cut dough into walnut-sized pieces; flatten with hand to oblong, 2½x2-inch pieces. Place 1 teaspoon filling in center. Fold over, pressing edges together in half moon shape. Place on cookie sheet lined with wax paper. Bake 30 minutes or until lightly browned.

Can be stored in glass container for about a week. Freezes well. May be topped with powdered sugar, a sugar and honey syrup or served plain.

Makes 70 to 80

PARVE   *Sephardic Dinner 2007*

Granny Lil Perlman's Heavenly Bits

1   cup butter
4   tablespoons powdered sugar
2   cups flour
1   tablespoon water
2   teaspoons vanilla
1   cup chopped pecans

Preheat oven to 350°. Mix butter, powdered sugar, flour, water and vanilla. Add pecans; mix well. Roll into small balls. Bake on greased baking sheet 20 minutes. When cooled, roll in additional powdered sugar.

I use a zipper plastic bag to coat cookies in powdered sugar.

DAIRY   *Carolyn Bern*

Grandma's Rugelach

1   (8 ounce) package cream cheese, room temperature
1   cup butter, room temperature
2½ cups sifted flour
1   cup powdered sugar or more for rolling

Choice of fillings - chopped nuts, egg white, sugar, cinnamon, combined to taste, or cinnamon/sugar, or apricot or strawberry jam

Preheat oven to 325°. Beat cream cheese and butter until smooth; mix in flour well. Gather dough into ball; wrap in plastic wrap; chill in refrigerator 7 hours. Roll out on board sprinkled with powdered sugar; sprinkle dough with powdered sugar. Roll out to about ⅛-inch thick, cut into 3-4-inch triangles. Spread each with chosen filling. Roll up beginning at base of triangles. Place on baking sheet point down, bend into crescent shape. Bake 15 minutes, until golden brown.

Be generous with powdered sugar; use as flour for rolling dough; there is no sugar in this dough.

DAIRY   *Helene Krupnick*

Granny Eva Ehrlich's Rugelach

1	(8 ounce) package cream cheese, softened	1/2	teaspoon salt
1	cup butter, softened		Cinnamon
2	cups flour		Sugar
			Chopped pecans

Cream together cream cheese and butter. Gradually add flour and salt, forming smooth dough. Wrap in wax paper; refrigerate overnight. Preheat oven to 350°. Split dough into three sections. While working with one section, return other sections to refrigerator. Roll dough into circle about 1/4-inch thick. Sprinkle with cinnamon, sugar and pecans. Cut into triangles and roll, starting at wide edge. Bake on ungreased cookie sheet 15-20 minutes. Remove to cooling rack. When completely cool, sprinkle with powdered sugar.

DAIRY   *Betty Ehrlich & Elaine Kirkpatrick*

Curabies – Sand Tart Cookies

1	cup sugar	1	tablespoon peanut butter
1	cup canola oil	2 1/2-3 cups White Lily all-purpose flour
1/2	teaspoon baking soda		Powdered sugar for dusting
1/2	teaspoon cinnamon		
1	cup ground nuts		

Preheat oven to 300°. Combine sugar, oil, baking soda and cinnamon; mix well. Add nuts and peanut butter; mix well. Add enough flour to hold mixture together. Knead and shape into walnut-size balls. Bake 30 minutes or until barely brown. Let cool; dust with powdered sugar.

This recipe is one my mother, Suzanna Varon, used to make. She always told me to add peanut butter to the recipe.

PARVE   *Alice Kleinberg*

Biscochos De Huevo Two – Plain Sugar Cookies

1   cup eggs
1   cup oil
1   cup sugar, heaping

1   teaspoon vanilla
2   teaspoons baking powder
6$\frac{1}{2}$-7 cups all-purpose flour, sifted

Preheat oven to 375°. Fill 1-cup measuring cup with eggs. Pour into electric mixer bowl; add oil, sugar and vanilla. Beat until well blended. Add baking powder. Add flour gradually; knead until dough is not sticky; add more flour as needed. Pinch walnut sized pieces; roll on surface with palms of hands into 5-inch rope, $\frac{1}{2}$-inch thick. Join ends to make circle. Brush with egg wash; place on wax paper lined baking sheet. Bake 12 minutes or until lightly brown. Remove from pans while warm. Reduce oven to 200°. Heap cookies on room-temperature pan; crisp 1 hour in oven. Completely cool before storing in air-tight container.

You can add a topping after you apply the egg-wash. Combine $\frac{1}{2}$ cup sugar and 1 teaspoon cinnamon. You may add finely chopped nuts to cinnamon mix or top with only nuts or sesame seeds. You can make this dough ahead, refrigerate overnight or freeze until ready to use.

PARVE   Jeanette C. Rousso

Reshas – Tea Biscuits

2	(.25 ounce) packages yeast		Dash cinnamon
2	cups warm water, divided	8-10	cups White Lily flour
1	cup + $\frac{1}{2}$ teaspoon sugar		Sesame seeds for sprinkling
1	cup oil		Cinnamon sugar for sprinkling

Dissolve yeast in $\frac{1}{2}$ cup warm water; add $\frac{1}{2}$ teaspoon sugar; set aside in warm place 10 minutes. Mix oil and 1 cup sugar; add cinnamon. Add yeast mixture.

Add flour gradually until dough is rather hard, not soft or sticky. Knead by hand or in mixer with dough hook until firm and smooth, similar to pie crust. Cover; rest in warm place 1 hour. Preheat oven to 350°. Turn dough out on floured board; knead lightly. Pinch a walnut-size piece of dough; roll into strip as thick as a pencil; shape into a pretzel; place on floured wax paper. Repeat for all dough. Rest reshas in warm place until double in size. Brush with beaten egg; sprinkle liberally with sesame seeds or cinnamon sugar. Set on lightly floured baking sheet. Bake 15-20 minutes, until lightly brown.

Remove from oven; reduce to 200°. Place reshas in overlapping rows on ungreased baking pans. Place in oven 1 hour or more until very crisp.

Store in air-tight containers. They freeze well.

Makes about 100

PARVE   *Pearl C. Hasson*

Tea Cake Cookies

1 cup butter, softened	5 cups all-purpose flour
2 cups sugar	1 teaspoon baking soda
3 eggs	1 teaspoon vanilla extract
2 tablespoons buttermilk	

Preheat oven to 400°. Cream butter; gradually add sugar, beating well. Add eggs, one at a time, beating well after each addition. Add buttermilk; beat well. Combine flour and baking soda; gradually stir into creamed mixture; stir in vanilla extract. Chill dough several hours or overnight. Roll dough to ¼-inch thickness on lightly floured surface. Cut into shapes with 3½-inch cookie cutter. Place 1 inch apart on lightly greased cookie sheets. Bake 7-8 minutes or until edges are lightly browned. Remove cookies to wire racks. Cool completely.

This recipe freezes well. You may substitute 1 teaspoon almond extract for vanilla. You may use the standard round shape or be creative for different occasions. These cookies can be decorated.

Makes 4 dozen

DAIRY   *Ruby Goldfield*

Crisp Sugar Cookies

½ cup butter	1 teaspoon vanilla
½ cup margarine	3 cups flour
1 cup sugar	1 teaspoon baking soda
1 egg, beaten	Additional sugar for sprinkling on top
½ teaspoon salt	

Preheat oven to 350°. Cream butter, margarine and sugar well. Add egg, salt and vanilla. Slowly add flour and baking soda. Mix well. Form into walnut-sized balls. Put on greased cookie sheet ½ inch apart. Flatten; sprinkle a little sugar on each. Bake 15 minutes. Remove from pan at once.

Makes about 100 cookies

DAIRY   *Linda Taffet*

Thumbprint Cookies

1   cup unsalted butter, room
      temperature
³/₄   cup sugar
¹/₂   teaspoon salt
2   large egg yolks

1   teaspoon vanilla extract
2¹/₄ cups all-purpose flour
      Raspberry preserves or jam, or
      flavor of choice

Beat butter, sugar and salt with electric mixer until light and fluffy. Add yolks, one at a time, scraping bowl after each addition; add vanilla. With mixer on low, add flour; mix just until combined. Wrap dough in plastic; chill 1 hour in refrigerator, until firm. Preheat oven to 350°. On parchment lined baking sheets, drop rounded teaspoons of cookie dough, 1 inch apart. Use finger or small measuring spoon to make a depression in center of each dough mound. Dip finger or spoon in flour if needed to keep from sticking. Fill each indentation with preserves or jam. Bake 10-15 minutes, until pale golden. Cool on wire racks.

Dough can be made ahead and refrigerated up to 2 weeks or frozen up to 3 months.

DAIRY   *Dana Handmacher*

Brownie Pie

2   squares unsweetened chocolate
½   cup unsalted butter
1   cup sugar
2   eggs, beaten
¼   cup flour
1   teaspoon vanilla
1   cup chopped nuts

Preheat oven to 325°. Combine chocolate and butter in medium saucepan; remove from heat. Stir in sugar, eggs, flour, vanilla and nuts. Coat pie pan, not deep dish, with cooking spray. Pour in filling. Bake 25-30 minutes. Serve with vanilla ice cream.

DAIRY   Dana Handmacher

Chocolate Pie

1   (3.75 ounce) package chocolate pudding mix, NOT instant
1   cup milk
1   (6 ounce) package semisweet chocolate chips
1   cup chopped pecans
1   (8 inch) graham cracker crust
1   cup whipping cream
2   tablespoons sugar

In medium saucepan, combine pudding mix and milk. Heat just to boil, stirring constantly. Remove from heat. Stir in chocolate chips and nuts. Stir to partially melt chips. Pour into crust. Put wax paper directly on pudding to prevent "skin" from forming. Cool completely several hours in refrigerator. Beat whipping cream with sugar until stiff. Remove wax paper from pie; top pie with whipped cream. Refrigerate.

DAIRY   Dana Handmacher

Elliot's Favorite Chocolate Pie

3 cups + 3 tablespoons all-purpose flour, more for rolling

½ teaspoon salt, divided

¾ cup shortening

⅓ cup orange juice

1½ squares unsweetened chocolate

1½ cups milk

¾ cup sugar, divided

3 tablespoons all-purpose flour

1 tablespoon cornstarch

¼ teaspoon salt

3 egg yolks, slightly beaten, reserve whites if topping with meringue

1 tablespoon butter

1 teaspoon vanilla

1 quart whipping cream

½ cup sugar

To make crust, pulse 3 cups flour and ¼ teaspoon salt in bowl of food processor with blade attachment. Add shortening; pulse until mixture resembles coarse meal. Add orange juice; pulse until dough starts to pull from sides of bowl. On lightly floured surface, divide dough in half; pat each into a disc. Wrap in plastic wrap; refrigerate 15 minutes. Remove and work one disc at a time. Place dough between 2 sheets wax paper. Roll out to 12-inch circle, about ⅛-inch thick. As you roll, add flour under dough as necessary, to prevent sticking. Transfer to 9-inch pie pan. Trim to ½-inch beyond edge of pan; fold under and flute edges. Prick bottom and sides all over. Line crust with aluminum foil, including edges. Fill at least two-thirds full with dry beans, rice, or stainless-steel pie weights. If making 2 pies, repeat with remaining disc; set aside. If only making 1 pie, wrap remaining disc well; freeze. Bake until edges of crust begin to turn golden and bottom has lost its translucent "raw" look, 10-12 minutes. Carefully pull up edge of foil to peek. Cool before filling.

To make filling, melt chocolate squares and milk in top of double boiler over boiling water. Remove from heat. Combine sugar, 3 tablespoons flour, corn starch and ¼ teaspoon salt; add to melted chocolate milk. Mix with wooden spoon. Gradually add egg yolks; blend in butter. Place over rapidly boiling water so pan is touching water. Cook 7 minutes or until thick and smooth, stirring constantly, scraping down sides of pan frequently. Remove from heat; add vanilla. Stir until smooth and blended, scraping sides of pan well. Pour hot filling into crust.

ELLIOT'S FAVORITE CHOCOLATE PIE, CONTINUED ON NEXT PAGE

ELLIOT'S FAVORITE CHOCOLATE PIE, CONTINUED

To make whipped cream topping, place whipping cream and sugar in mixer; beat until stiff peaks form. Spread on top of pie. To make meringue, preheat oven to 350°. Use reserved egg whites; must be room temperature. In a medium glass or metal bowl whip egg whites until foamy. Gradually add ¼ cup sugar, continuing to beat until whites form stiff peaks. Spread meringue over pie, covering completely. Bake in preheated oven 5-6 minutes, until meringue is golden brown. Chill before serving.

Double filling amounts to make 2 pies. To make a vanilla pie, omit chocolate; decrease sugar to ½ cup.

DAIRY   *Mae Cohen*

Frozen Hawaiian Pie

1 (12 ounce) container frozen whipped topping, thawed	1 (11 ounce) can Mandarin orange segments, drained
1 (14 ounce) can Eagle Brand milk	¾ cup flaked coconut
1 (20 ounce) can crushed pineapple, drained	½ cup chopped toasted pecans
2 tablespoons lemon juice	½ cup pitted Bing cherries
½ cup mashed ripe banana	2 (9 inch) graham cracker crusts
	Mint sprigs for garnish

Reserve 3 tablespoons whipped topping. Stir together remaining whipped topping and milk. Fold in pineapple, lemon juice, banana, orange, ½ cup coconut, pecans and cherries. Pour evenly into crusts. Cover; freeze 12 hours or until firm. Remove from freezer; let stand 10 minutes before serving. Garnish with remaining coconut, mint sprigs and reserved whipped topping.

Serves 16

DAIRY   *Bonnie London*

Chewy Coconut Chess Pie

5	eggs	2	teaspoons vanilla
1½	cups sugar	½	teaspoon salt
½	cup butter, melted	1½	cups flaked coconut
1	tablespoon vinegar	1	(9 inch) unbaked pie shell

Preheat oven to 325°. In medium bowl, beat together eggs, sugar, melted butter, vinegar, vanilla and salt until well blended; stir in coconut. Pour into pie shell. Bake 50-60 minutes or until knife inserted near center comes out clean. Cool on wire rack. Serve with vanilla ice cream, if desired.

Serves 8

DAIRY   *Robin Blitz*

Hint of Orange Pumpkin Pie

1	frozen deep dish pie crust	⅓	cup sweet orange marmalade
1	(16 ounce) can pumpkin	1	tablespoon pumpkin pie spice
1	(14 ounce) can Eagle Brand milk	½	teaspoon salt
2	eggs		

Preheat oven to 400°. Place crust on baking sheet. Beat pumpkin, Eagle Brand milk, eggs, marmalade, pumpkin pie spice and salt until blended; pour into crust. Bake 50-55 minutes or until knife inserted comes out clean.

Serves 8

DAIRY   *Jo Anne H. Rousso*

Sylvia Stamm's Southern Pecan Pie

1	cup light brown sugar, packed	1	teaspoon vanilla
1	cup light corn syrup	1½	cups pecans
3	eggs	1	(9 inch) unbaked pie shell

Preheat oven to 350°. Mix brown sugar, syrup, eggs and vanilla by hand; stir in pecans. Pour into pie shell. Bake on cookie sheet 20 minutes. Reduce heat to 300°; bake 30-40 minutes. Pie is done when it won't "shake" in pie shell.

This recipe was a favorite of our mother, Sylvia Segall Stamm. She delighted her husband Abe's Yankee family with this pie for almost 50 years. She also had the pleasure of later spoiling her Chicago "machatunim" (daughter Donna's in-laws) with it as well. Talk about spreading Southern hospitality!

PARVE   *Donna Stamm Speigel, Mitch Stamm & Susan Stamm*

Maxine's Quick Peach Cobbler

½	cup margarine	1	cup sugar
1	cup self-rising flour	2	(15 ounce) cans peaches in heavy syrup
1	cup milk		

Preheat oven to 350°. Melt margarine in baking dish. Mix flour, milk and sugar. Pour mixture on top of margarine. DO NOT STIR. Drain off about ½ of syrup and pour peaches on top. Bake 1 hour.

DAIRY   *Carol Capouano*

Meringue Banana Pudding

³/₄	cup granulated sugar, divided	2	cups milk
¹/₃	cup all-purpose flour	¹/₂	teaspoon vanilla extract
	Dash salt	35-45	vanilla wafer cookies, divided
4	eggs separated, room temperature	5-6	medium size full ripe bananas, sliced, divided

Preheat oven to 425°. Combine ¹/₂ cup sugar, flour and salt in top of double boiler. Stir in 4 egg yolks and milk. Blend well. Cook uncovered over boiling water, stirring constantly, until thickened. Reduce heat; cook 5 minutes, stirring occasionally. Remove from heat; add vanilla; let cool. Spread small amount on bottom of 1¹/₂-quart or 9x9 baking dish. Reserve 1 banana and 12 cookies for garnish. Cover with layer of vanilla wafers; then a layer of sliced bananas. Pour ¹/₄ of custard over bananas. Continue to layer wafers, bananas and custard to make 3 layers of each, ending with custard on top. In a separate bowl, whip egg whites with electric mixer to soft peaks. Gradually sprinkle remaining ¹/₄ cup sugar while continuing to whip until stiff firm peaks form. Spread egg whites over top and to edges of casserole, making swirls with peaks on top. Bake 5-8 minutes until meringue has browned. Watch carefully; do not burn meringue. Garnish edge of baking dish with bananas and wafers before serving. Serve warm or at room temperature.

Cover with plastic wrap and refrigerate any remaining pudding.

This is one of my favorite dishes from my mother, Selma Capouya Capouano.

DAIRY   *Anita Capouano*

Roasted Banana Pudding

5	unpeeled ripe bananas	1½	tablespoons butter
3	cups low-fat milk	1	tablespoon vanilla extract
1	cup sugar, divided	1	(12 ounce) container low-fat whipped topping, thawed, divided
3	tablespoons cornstarch		
¼	teaspoon salt	30	vanilla wafers
3	large eggs		

Preheat oven to 350°. Place bananas on cookie sheet lined with parchment paper. Bake 40 minutes. Carefully peel and mash in small bowl; set aside. In saucepan, combine milk and ½ cup sugar over medium-high heat. Reduce to simmer. In medium bowl, combine remaining sugar, cornstarch, salt and eggs; stir with whisk. GRADUALLY add egg mixture to hot mixture, raise heat to medium; cook, stirring constantly until thickened; remove from heat. Add bananas, butter and vanilla; stir. Fold in 3 tablespoons whipped topping. Layer pudding and vanilla wafers in serving dish. Top with remaining whipped topping.

DAIRY   *Sandi Stern*

Sheri Blondheim Weiner's Banana Pudding

1	(3.4 ounce) box instant vanilla pudding	1	(12 ounce) container Cool Whip
3	cups whole milk	2	(12 ounce) boxes vanilla wafers
1	(14 ounce) can Eagle Brand milk	6-8	bananas

Make pudding with whole milk; add Eagle Brand milk; add Cool Whip. Line large bowl with wafers. Add layer of sliced bananas. Add layer of pudding. Add layer of wafers. Continue layers, ending with pudding. Refrigerate at least 2 hours before serving.

Serves 12

DAIRY   *Diane K. Blondheim*

Ida Raymon's Rice Pudding

1	cup rice	Juice of ½ lemon
2	eggs, separated	1¼ cups milk
½	cup sugar	½ cup butter

Preheat oven to 350°. Boil rice 15 minutes; rinse in hot water. Add 2 egg yolks; add sugar and lemon juice. Melt butter in milk; add to rice. Beat egg whites; fold into rice. Pour into greased 8x8 baking dish. Bake 1 hour.

This pudding makes a little topping as it cooks. The topping can turn brown easily so turn down the temperature if this starts to happen. We have also made this pudding using a whole cup of sugar and a teaspoon of vanilla. We have also made it without beating the whites and using 1 package of instant rice instead of long cooking rice. The recipe is very forgiving. Try it the original way first.

Serves 4

This is a simple, warm, comforting rice pudding that my mother made when I was growing up.

DAIRY *Edward Raymon*

Celebrations...

High Holidays

Chanukah

Purim

Passover

The strength of the Jewish home — the glue that holds the household together — is a commitment to faith and in particular the Jewish Holidays. Every family has its own special recipes and food traditions for our special holidays and festivals. Our Sisterhood members are pleased to share some of their favorites for you to enjoy.

Honey Cake – One

½ cup slivered almonds

1 box pudding-in-the-mix yellow
   cake mix

1 teaspoon cinnamon

1 teaspoon ginger

1 cup honey

¾ cup strong brewed coffee or
   2 teaspoons instant coffee
   dissolved in ¾ cup water, cold

⅓ cup oil

2 tablespoons grated orange peel

1 tablespoon grated lemon peel

3 eggs

Preheat oven to 325°. Grease and flour Bundt pan. Sprinkle almonds in pan.
Combine dry cake mix, cinnamon, ginger, honey, cold coffee, oil, orange peel,
lemon peel and eggs at low speed until moistened. Beat 2 minutes at highest
speed. Pour into pan. Bake 45 minutes or until toothpick inserted in center
comes out clean. Cool upright in pan 15 minutes. Invert onto serving plate.

DAIRY *Elaine Kirkpatrick*

My Mother's Honey Cake for Rosh Hashanah

2½ cups flour

2 teaspoons baking powder

½ teaspoon cloves

½ teaspoon ginger

1 teaspoon baking soda

2 teaspoons cinnamon

1 cup oil

1 cup sugar

1 cup honey

1 cup hot black coffee

3 eggs, beaten

Preheat oven to 325°. Sift flour, baking powder, cloves, ginger, baking soda
and cinnamon; set aside. Blend oil with sugar; add honey, then coffee; stir.
Gradually add eggs. Blend in dry ingredients. Bake 1 hour.

Makes 4 loaf pans or 1 Bundt pan

PARVE *Esther B. Labovitz*

Honey Cake – Two

1³/₄ cups all-purpose flour

1 teaspoon cinnamon

³/₄ teaspoon baking soda

³/₄ teaspoon salt

¹/₂ teaspoon baking powder

1 cup honey

²/₃ cup vegetable oil

¹/₂ cup strong coffee

2 eggs

¹/₄ cup packed brown sugar

2 tablespoons whiskey

¹/₂ cup chopped walnuts

2 tablespoons powdered sugar

Preheat oven to 350°. Spray Bundt pan with cooking spray. Whisk flour, cinnamon, baking soda, salt and baking powder. In a separate bowl, whisk honey, oil and coffee. In large electric mixer bowl, beat eggs and brown sugar 3 minutes at high speed. Reduce speed to low; add honey mixture and whiskey. Mix 1 minute or until blended. Add flour mixture and walnuts. Pour into pan. Bake 45 minutes or until wooden toothpick comes out clean. Turn onto cake plate to cool. Dust with powdered sugar; serve.

The first time I hosted Rosh Hashanah in our home, I was concerned that I would not have enough traditional items on my menu. To my surprise, my Honey Cake was the hit of the menu!

PARVE   *Rebecca Robison Ternus*

Sweet Holiday Vegetable Tzimmes

3-4	medium sweet potatoes		1⅓	cups butter
1	(2 pound) bag carrots		1	cup brown sugar
1	(8-10 ounce) bag dried prunes		1	cup dark corn syrup
1	(8-10 ounce) bag dried apricots			

Preheat oven to 350°. Peel and slice sweet potatoes or cut into big chucks. Peel and cut carrots into large pieces. Put in large pot; cover with water. Boil 20 minutes or until tender. Drain water from pot; keep vegetables in pot. Add prunes and apricots. Cover; steam 3-5 minutes to plump up dried fruit. In saucepan, cook butter, brown sugar and corn syrup over low heat until just boiling. Pour over vegetables and fruit. Put in greased 8x8 dish; bake 20-30 minutes until hot and bubbly.

Serves 6 to 8

PARVE   *Elaine L. Raymon*

Edible Dreidels

1	(size of your choice) bag chocolate candy kisses		1	(size of your choice) bag large marshmallows
1	small jar smooth peanut butter, not crunchy		1	(size of your choice) bag thin pretzel sticks

Unwrap kisses; set aside. Spread a finger-full of peanut butter on top of a marshmallow. Press bottom of a kiss into peanut butter. Hold marshmallow by sides; poke pretzel stick through other end until it touches the kiss. Place on plate so tip of kiss is the spinner and pretzel is dreidel handle.

When they were all children, our son's friends came over every year to line up and make these cute little dreidels...a family Chanukah tradition that I hope to pass down to my grandchildren!

DAIRY   *Rhonda Blitz*

Burmuelos – Chanukah Fritters

4 teaspoons yeast	1½ cups sugar
3½ cups warm water, divided	1½ cups honey
Pinch of salt	Oil for frying
3 cups White Lily all-purpose flour	Cinnamon sugar topping, optional
1 egg	

Soften yeast in ½ cup warm water. In mixing bowl, combine salt and flour. Add yeast mixture, egg and 1½ cups water; mix well. Cover bowl; place in warm place 2 hours. To make syrup, combine sugar, honey and 1½ cups water in saucepan. Boil until sticky. Cool before pouring over burmuelos. To fry burmuelos, fill 2-quart pot with 3 inches oil; heat to very hot. Carefully drop teaspoon-size pieces of dough into hot oil. Fry until golden brown; remove with slotted spoon; drain on paper towels. Serve with syrup or sprinkle with cinnamon sugar topping, if using.

PARVE *Traditional Sephardic Recipe*

Quick Burmuelos – Chanukah Fritters

1 egg	1½ cups honey
1 cup milk	1½ cups water
1 teaspoon baking powder	Oil for frying
1½ cups flour	Cinnamon sugar topping, optional
1½ cups sugar	

Beat egg; add milk; beat again. Mix flour and baking powder; gradually add to egg mixture. Mix until blended. To make syrup, combine sugar, honey and water in saucepan. Bring to boil; reduce heat; simmer until sticky. Cool before pouring over hot burmuelos. To fry burmuelos, fill 2-quart pot with 3 inches oil; heat to very hot. Drop batter by tablespoonfuls into oil. Fry until golden brown; remove with slotted spoon; drain on paper towels. Serve with syrup or cinnamon sugar topping.

DAIRY *Traditional Sephardic Recipe*

Sylvia Stamm's Dreidel Cookies – Cookie Wheels

1	egg	1	tablespoon sugar
½	cup milk	½	teaspoon salt
1	tablespoon vegetable oil + more as needed for heating rosette iron	½	cup all-purpose flour
			Powdered sugar for sprinkling

Beat egg slightly; add milk and oil; gradually add sugar, salt and flour; beat until smooth. Heat 3-4 inches oil to 400° in saucepan. Heat rosette iron in hot oil; get iron very hot. Dip iron into batter until two-thirds covered; quickly immerse iron into hot oil; fry until golden brown. Remove from oil. Gently push cookie from iron; invert on paper towel on cookie sheet. Repeat dipping/frying process; occasionally stir batter. Sprinkle with powdered sugar.

Makes 3 to 4 dozen

We are proud to honor the memory of our mother, Sylvia Segall Stamm, a lifelong member of Agudath Israel and Sisterhood by sharing her recipes. Her delicious cookies and cakes influenced my brother Mitch, who is now a professional baking instructor. An article about this recipe was published in The Montgomery Advertiser in 1979. It featured photos of my mother preparing this recipe with my sister, Susan and me. The rosette iron my mother used belonged to her mother, Esther Segall, also a devoted Sisterhood member. Dreidel cookies are a treat we remember fondly!

DAIRY   Mitch Stamm, Susan Stamm & Donna Stamm Speigel

Grandma Herman's Potato Pancakes

2	large baking potatoes	1/2	cup flour or matzah meal
2	eggs		Salt, to taste
2	tablespoons water		Pepper, to taste
1/2	teaspoon baking powder		Butter for frying

Grate potatoes. Drain out potato water. Add water. Add eggs; beat in. Add flour or matzah meal to thicken. Add salt and pepper. Stir. Add baking powder. Fry in butter.

Serves 4

PARVE

Robert, William & Joanna Shujman,
great-grandchildren of Grandma Anne Gardner Herman

Potato Latkes

8	large baking potatoes	1/4	teaspoon garlic powder
2	eggs	1/4	teaspoon salt
1	large Bermuda onion		Vegetable oil

Put potatoes in food processor; grate to very fine. Add eggs. Add onion; process until totally blended to fine consistency. Add garlic powder and salt. Heat oil in skillet until very hot. Place well-filled tablespoons potato mixture in skillet. Fry until golden brown.

PARVE

Sandy Segall

Shortcut Potato Latkes

1	box Steits or Manischewitz Potato Pancake Latke Mix	2	cups finely chopped onion, optional
4	large eggs		Canola oil for frying
1	(20 ounce) bag Simply Potatoes Unseasoned Shredded Hash Browns		Applesauce
			Sour cream, optional

Each box contains 2 bags of mix. Use both bags. In large bowl, combine mix with eggs according to directions on box. Let stand 10 minutes. Add entire bag of potatoes; stir well. Add onions if using; stir well. Heat oil in large skillet until drop of water dropped in oil bubbles up. Use large spoon to gently place potato mixture in oil. When brown, use spatula and spoon to turn, so oil does not pop. When both sides are brown, remove from oil; place on brown bags covered with paper towels to drain. Remove small fried pieces from oil as necessary; change oil if it turns dark.

Look for hash browns in dairy case or near eggs. I also use frozen chopped onions. Serve with applesauce. Serve sour cream too, if it is a dairy meal. Latkes can be made ahead of time, stored in refrigerator or freezer; bring to room temperature, reheat uncovered in 350° oven.

Makes 20 to 25 latkes

This is my shortcut recipe and it is so easy !!!! I almost hate to share it, but it is a fail proof recipe. I use it to make the latkes every year at the synagogue and they are enjoyed by all. Most people think it is a fancy complicated recipe. Not true...I don't even grate my own potatoes! So now my secret is out and I am happy to share it with our cookbook readers.

PARVE OR DAIRY   *Esther C. Miller*

Sweet Potato Latkes

3   medium sweet potatoes, about
    1 pound, peeled
1   large onion
1   tablespoon chili powder
2   eggs
1/2   teaspoon salt

1/8   teaspoon black pepper
3   heaping tablespoons potato
    starch
1/2   cup vegetable oil
    Sour cream, optional

Fit food processor with shredding disc. Shred sweet potatoes; place in colander. Shred onion; toss with sweet potatoes. Drain 10 minutes. Transfer to large bowl. Whisk together chili powder, eggs, salt and pepper. Stir into sweet potato mixture; mix well. In large nonstick skillet, heat oil over medium-high heat. Place 6 mounds of mixture (about 1/4 cup each) into skillet. Press down lightly. Sauté until browned, about 2-3 minutes per side. Drain on baking sheet lined with paper towels. Sprinkle lightly with salt to taste. Serve with sour cream, if desired.

PARVE OR DAIRY   *Rhonda Blitz*

Hamantaschen

¾ cup sugar

¾ cup oil

1 teaspoon vanilla

4 eggs

1 teaspoon baking powder

4-5 cups all-purpose soft winter wheat baking flour

Fruit preserves for filling, flavor of your choice

Preheat oven to 350°. Mix sugar, oil, vanilla, eggs and baking powder. Gradually add flour until dough is texture of cookie dough. Roll out small portions of dough on lightly floured surface. Use 2-inch round cookie cutter to cut dough. Put a dollop of filling in middle. Do not put too much filling; it will overflow. Pinch to make a triangle. Make sure sides are pinched closed and seams sealed to prevent cookies from opening up during baking. Put on cookie sheets sprayed with cooking oil. Bake 15-20 minutes, until the bottoms are golden brown.

My fondest memories are making these cookies with Jean Hauben and Lil Perlman every year for the synagogue's Purim celebration. They were true Matriarchs of our kitchen and Sisterhood. They taught me so much!

PARVE

Sharon Allen

Emily's Charoset

5	apples, peeled, cored, cut into chunks	1½-2	cups chopped pecans or walnuts
2	(10.5 ounce) packages pitted dates	¼	cup white vinegar, or to taste

Put apples and dates in large pot; barely cover with water. Cook until apples are tender and most of water is evaporated. Put into blender or food processor; blend until mixture is like a thick spread. Add nuts and vinegar. Stir to mix all ingredients well. Chill.

PARVE *Emily Allen*

Diane's Charoset

2	apples, peeled, cored, chopped	1	cup chopped pecans
2	tablespoons honey	1	cup dried currents
½	cup grape concord wine	1	cup pitted dates, coarsely chopped
1	cup chopped untoasted almonds	1	teaspoon cinnamon
½	cup chopped walnuts		

Mix apples, honey, wine, almonds, walnuts, pecans, currents, dates and cinnamon.

May be made up to 2 days ahead. Refrigerate to store.

PARVE *Diane K. Blondheim*

Barbara's Charoset

2   apples, peeled, cored
1   cup nuts, any variety

1   teaspoon cinnamon
⅓   cup wine

Chop apples and nuts. Add cinnamon and wine. Mix all ingredients together. Chill.

Leftover charoset may be kept in refrigerator at least a week. Delicious when added to a matzah kugel.

PARVE   *Barbara Handmacher*

Pearl's Charoset

5   cooking apples, peeled, cored, chopped
4   cups dates
    Water to cover
2   cups ground almonds, pecans and/or walnuts

1   cup vinegar
⅛   cup reserved liquid
½   cup sweet red wine, to taste

Put apples and dates in large pot. Add enough water to just cover fruit. Boil 15 minutes or until apples are tender. Drain, reserving liquid; let cool. Process fruit in food processor, pulsing 3-4 times; it should be finely chopped, not puréed. Remove to large bowl. Add ground nuts to fruit. Add vinegar, fruit liquid and wine. Stir until well blended. Add reserved fruit juice as needed to obtain your desired consistency. Chill before serving.

Keeps 2 to 3 weeks in refrigerator.

PARVE   *Pearl C. Hasson*

Rebbetzin Irene's Charoset

1	cup nuts, walnuts, pecans, almonds or all three	3	tablespoons sweet wine or sweet grape juice, more to taste
5	apples, peeled, cored	3	tablespoons sugar
1	teaspoon grated lemon peel	2	teaspoons cinnamon
			Dash of ginger

Insert metal blade in food processor; add nuts. Chop nuts with 1 or 2 pulses. Cut apples into 1-inch pieces; add to processor. Add wine or grape juice, sugar, cinnamon and ginger. Pulse several times until everything is medium-fine. Scrape sides of processor with spatula; check for large pieces under blade. Adjust seasonings to taste; remove from processor. Cover; refrigerate.

This is usually the last dish I make the night before our first seder. I make 2 versions, one with wine and one with grape juice, since some of our visitors don't drink wine. I make plenty so it can be served as a side dish with leftovers.

PARVE   *Irene E. Kramer*

Marilyn Rosen's Charoset

1	apple	2	packets sweetener
1	orange	3-4	dates
¼	cup raisins		Cinnamon, to taste
¼	cup unsalted peanuts or pecans		

Core and coarsely chop apple. Peel, section and seed orange. Use food processor to blend apple, orange, raisins, nuts, sweetener and dates until finely chopped. Sprinkle cinnamon over mixture, re-cover and re-blend. Refrigerate 1 hour or more.

PARVE   *Linda Smith*

Richard's Charoset

Apples, peeled
Wine to taste
Plenty of honey

Plenty of chopped pecans
Plenty of cinnamon......I mean
PLENTY!

Place apples in food processor; chop until medium fine. Drain in colander; squeeze out juice. Transfer to bowl, add wine, honey, pecans and cinnamon. Stir to mix all ingredients. Chill; serve.

PARVE   *Richard Shinbaum*

Apple-Matzah Kugel

4 large Granny Smith or other tart apples, cored, medium diced
$1/2$ cup light brown sugar
$1/4$ cup orange juice
6 plain matzah
8 eggs
1 teaspoon salt

$1^1/2$ cups sugar, adjust to taste
1 teaspoon ground cinnamon
$3/4$ cup butter or margarine, divided
$1^1/2$ cups golden raisins
1 cup dried apricots, medium chopped

Preheat oven to 350°. Toss apples with brown sugar and orange juice; set aside in a bowl. Break matzah into 2-3-inch pieces; soak in a cup of warm water until soft but not mushy, set aside. While matzah soaks, melt $1/2$ cup butter; set aside. Beat eggs with whisk in large bowl; add salt, sugar, cinnamon and melted butter. Add apples mixture, raisins and apricots. Squeeze liquid from softened matzah; add to egg mixture. Stir kugel well; pour into lightly greased $2^1/2$-quart or 10x14 baking dish. Dot top with $1/4$ cup butter. Bake 1 hour. Cover top with foil if browns too early.

This can be made up to 2 days ahead. Cool before refrigerating, covered. Bring to room temperature; reheat, uncovered at 350°.

Serves 12

PARVE   *Margie Allen & Carolyn Bern*

Burmuelos – Farfel Pancakes

2 cups farfel, more as needed	1/4 cup feta cheese
2 eggs, more as needed	1 1/2 cups grated Romano cheese, more to taste
1/2 teaspoon salt	
Pepper to taste	Peanut oil for frying
1/4 cup cottage cheese	

Soak farfel in water; drain; squeeze dry. Beat eggs; add salt, pepper, and all cheeses. Add farfel or eggs as needed so mixture holds shape when dropped into hot oil. Drop by tablespoons into oil. Fry until golden brown. Drain on paper towels.

Serve with grated Romano cheese, sour cream, preserves, fruit relishes, honey, and/or fresh fruit.

My Passover Matzah Pancake Indoor Picnic started when my in-town grandchildren, Eli and Jeanine were young. Since Sunday School didn't meet during Passover, it was a perfect time for brunch with Grandma and Papoo. It began as a no frills, simple meal. Over the years, it has become a much anticipated, major friends and extended family get-together for more than 50 people, with a much expanded menu.

DAIRY

Jeanette C. Rousso

Keftes de Prassa – Leek Patties

3	cups leeks	1	teaspoon salt
3	spring onions		Pepper to taste
1	cup mashed potatoes	2	tablespoons matzah meal
3	eggs, beaten		Peanut oil for frying

Wash, chop and cook leeks and spring onions in water. Drain; put in large bowl. Add potatoes, eggs, salt, pepper and matzah meal; stir. Shape into small patties. Fry in oil until golden brown on both sides.

PARVE   *Jeanette C. Rousso*

Baked Cheese Matzah

5-6	sheets matzah	4	cups cottage cheese
1/4	cup butter, melted	1/4	cup matzah meal, or more
1/3	cup sugar	1/2	teaspoon salt
4	eggs		Cinnamon sugar for sprinkling

Preheat oven to 350°. Moisten matzah sheets. Spray 9x13 pan with cooking spray; line with matzah. Mix butter, sugar and eggs; add cottage cheese, matzah meal and salt; mix well. Add more matzah meal if mixture is too soupy. Spread mixture over matzah. Sprinkle with cinnamon sugar. Bake 20 minutes or until center is set.

DAIRY   *Naomi Gold, wife of Rabbi Raphael Gold, a former rabbi.*

Matzah Brei

2   eggs
½   slice matzah soaked in ¼ cup
     milk

1   slice American cheese, crumbled
2   tablespoons butter, for frying

Beat eggs. Add cheese. Fold in matzah. Fry in butter until lightly browned on bottom. Flip matzah brei; brown on other side. Top with jam or jelly, if desired.

DAIRY   *Esther B. Labovitz*

Matzah Rolls

²⁄₃   cup water
¹⁄₃   cup vegetable oil, not corn oil
1   tablespoon sugar

1   teaspoon salt
1   cup matzah meal
3   eggs

Preheat oven 350° to 375°. Bring water, oil, sugar and salt to a boil. Add matzah meal; stir into mixture. Add eggs one at a time; mix well. Remove from heat. Form into 12 rolls. Bake on a greased baking sheet 45 minutes.

Since this recipe has been handed down in my husband's family for years and predates the accuracy of our current appliances, the actual baking time and temperature are approximate. This was one of the first recipes my mother-in-law, Blanche Sass, gave to me after we got married. It is always a big hit at our house.

PARVE   *Paige Sass*

Matzah Bagels

²/₃	cup water	1	teaspoon salt
¹/₃	cup oil	1	cup matzah meal
1	tablespoon sugar	3	eggs

Preheat oven to 350°. In saucepan combine water, oil, sugar and salt. Bring to boil; stir. Remove from heat; add matzah meal. Mix until moist. Add eggs one at a time; mix between each addition. Plop large spoonfuls of dough onto a greased cookie sheet. Use wet fingers to make a hole in middle of each plop. Bake 40-45 minutes.

PARVE   *Marsha Orange*

Ruth Segall's Low Fat Matzah Balls

3	eggs, separated	¹/₂	teaspoon salt
³/₄	cup matzah meal	3	quarts water

Place egg whites in mixer bowl; whip on high speed until stiff. In another bowl, combine egg yolks, matzah meal and salt; mix well. Gently fold egg whites into matzah meal mixture. Refrigerate 30 minutes. Bring 3 quarts water to a rolling boil, then reduce heat. Wet hands; form mixture into 10 or 12 balls. Drop into simmering water. Cover; simmer 20 minutes. Transfer matzah balls to hot soup to serve.

PARVE   *Sisterhood Recipe Swap*

Rebbetzin Irene's Chicken Soup with Matzah Balls

1	(3-4 pound) skinned chicken, cut in 8ths, or 2-3 pounds skinless chicken breasts
4	quarts water
1	onion, chopped
2	large carrots, chopped
2	stalks celery, with leaves, chopped
	A few sprigs fresh dill, chopped or $^1/_4$ teaspoon dried dill
	A few sprigs fresh parsley, chopped or 1 tablespoon dried parsley
1-1$^1/_2$	tablespoons salt
2	tablespoons instant dry chicken broth granules
$^1/_4$	teaspoon white pepper
$^1/_4$	teaspoon garlic powder
3	bay leaves
2	eggs
2	tablespoons vegetable oil
$^1/_4$-$^1/_2$	teaspoon salt
$^1/_2$-$^3/_4$	cup matzah meal
2	tablespoons water
1$^1/_2$	quarts water

Place chicken pieces, 4 quarts water, onion, carrots, celery, dill, parsley, salt, broth granules, pepper, garlic power and bay leaves in a large soup kettle. Bring to boil, lower heat; simmer, covered, 1 hour or until chicken is tender. Remove bay leaves. Remove chicken; bone; return to pot. While soup is simmering, make matzah balls. Beat eggs, oil and $^1/_4$-$^1/_2$ teaspoon salt together with fork. Blend in matzah meal with fork to make a stiff mixture. Add 2 tablespoons water; mix again. Cover; refrigerate 15 minutes. Remove matzah mixture; with moistened hands, form into 1-inch balls. Bring 1$^1/_2$ quarts water to boil in large pot. Add matzah balls to boiling water; bring back to a boil. Lower heat; boil 45 minutes. Remove from water; add to soup. DO NOT cook matzah balls in soup.

Serves 10 to 12

Since I was not brought up Jewish, when the Rabbi and I were newly-weds over 30 years ago, I wanted to learn how to cook some Jewish dishes. This soup was my first try. It has been a constant at our Shabbat table and I have passed the recipe down to all three of our children. It brings a smile to my face when I hear they have become "famous" in their social circles because of their chicken soup and matzah balls.

MEAT

Irene E. Kramer

Megina – Meat Pie

2	tablespoons oil	5	eggs, divided
¾	cup chopped onion	3	hard-boiled eggs
2	pounds ground beef	1	cup fresh chopped parsley
2	teaspoons salt	2	cups farfel
1	teaspoon pepper	½	cup chicken broth

Preheat oven to 400°. Brown onion and beef in oil. Add salt and pepper. Simmer until well done. Remove from heat; drain excess grease. Add 3 beaten eggs and 3 chopped hard-boiled eggs. Add parsley; mix well. Soak farfel in warm water until soft; drain; squeeze dry. Beat 2 eggs; mix with farfel. Put thin layer of farfel in bottom of greased 9x13 baking dish. Pour meat mixture over farfel layer. Top with rest of farfel. Bake 30 minutes. After removing from oven, pour chicken broth over top before serving.

__MEAT__   *Jeanette C. Rousso*

Burmuelos de Patata – Potato Pancakes

4	large potatoes, peeled, boiled, mashed	3	eggs, beaten
½	cup matzah meal	1	teaspoon salt
1½	cups grated Romano cheese, more to taste		Peanut oil for frying

Stir potatoes, matzah meal, cheese, eggs and salt just until mixed. Add eggs, potatoes or matzah meal as needed; mixture should hold shape when dropped into hot oil. Drop by tablespoonfuls; fry until golden brown on both sides.

__DAIRY__   *Jeanette C. Rousso*

Passover Quajado De Carne – Meat Casserole

2	pounds ground beef	1	teaspoon pepper
2	tablespoons oil	1/4	cup chopped parsley
1	cup farfel, soaked in warm water, squeezed dry	10	eggs
1	tablespoon salt	1	medium potato, mashed

Brown beef in oil; cool. Add salt, pepper, parsley and farfel. Add 2 beaten eggs at a time to mixture until 8 eggs have been used. Grease 9x13 baking dish; heat in oven 2-3 minutes. Pour mixture into pan; beat 2 eggs with mashed potato; spread over top. Bake 30 minutes or until golden brown.

For added flavor, brown 1 chopped onion with meat. You may omit mashed potato and spread 2 beaten eggs on top.

MEAT   *Traditional Sephardic Recipe*

Passover Quajado De Spinaca – Passover Spinach Quajado

2	pounds fresh spinach, washed, cut, drained	1/2	cup farfel, soaked in warm water, squeezed dry
6	eggs, beaten	1/2	cup cottage cheese
1	cup grated Parmesan or Romano cheese	2	teaspoons salt
		1/4	cup oil

Preheat oven to 400°. Pour oil into 9x9 baking dish; heat pan in oven 2-3 minutes. Mix spinach, eggs, cheese, farfel, cottage cheese and salt thoroughly. Pour into heated pan; bake 25 minutes, or until set and beginning to pull away from edges of pan.

DAIRY   *Traditional Sephardic Recipe*

Delicious Passover Brownies

4	eggs	½	cup matzah cake meal, sifted
2	cups sugar	½	cup potato starch
1	cup oil	½	teaspoon salt
4	tablespoons cocoa	2	cups pecans

Preheat oven to 325°. Mix eggs, sugar, oil, cocoa, matzah meal, potato starch and salt together, either in a food processor or mixer. Stir in pecans. Pour batter into greased 9x13 pan. Bake 35-40 minutes.

PARVE   *Teri Aronou*

Matzah Brownies

4	ounces unsweetened chocolate	1	cup matzah cake meal
½	cup margarine	¼	teaspoon salt
2	cups sugar	½	cup chopped nuts
4	eggs		Powdered sugar for sprinkling on top
1	tablespoon brandy or water		

Preheat oven to 350°. Melt chocolate and margarine over low heat. Stir together chocolate mixture and sugar in mixer bowl. Beat in eggs, one at a time on medium speed. Stir in brandy/water, cake meal, salt and nuts. Pour into a greased 9x9 baking pan. Bake 30 minutes. When cool, sprinkle with powdered sugar.

Serves 12

DAIRY   *Jeanette C. Rousso*

Nut Cake for Passover

12	eggs	½	cup white kosher wine
2	cups sugar	1½	heaping cups matzah cake meal
1	lemon, zested, juiced	1	cup chopped walnuts

Preheat oven to 325°. Separate 8 eggs. Beat yolks and 4 whole eggs with sugar until creamy. Add lemon zest, juice and wine; mix. Add cake meal and nuts; mix; set aside. Beat egg whites until stiff peaks form; fold into batter. Pour batter into greased 10-inch tube cake pan. Bake 1 hour-1 hour 10 minutes. Do not undercook. Remove from oven; invert pan on a bottle so that top of pan is at least 6 inches above countertop. It will rise as it cools. Completely cool upside down; turn right side up; run flexible metal spatula around edges to loosen; remove from pan.

I serve this with Lemon Curd. You may also serve with sliced, sweetened strawberries or other berries.

PARVE   *Pearl C. Hasson*

Passover Sponge Cake

9	eggs	¾	tablespoon lemon juice and grated rind
1¾	cups sugar, divided		
	Pinch of salt	¾	cup potato starch
		¼	cup matzah cake flour

Preheat oven to 325°. Separate 7 eggs. Beat whites until almost stiff. Add ½ cup sugar to whites. Continue to beat. Add salt. Beat egg yolks and 2 whole eggs with remaining sugar. Beat until thick and is a lemony color. Add lemon juice and rind. Sift potato starch and matzah cake flour. Add to yolk mixture; fold in egg whites. Bake in tube pan 1 hour. Turn upside down to cool.

PARVE   *Sandi Stern*

Passover Chocolate Roll

Unsweetened cocoa to dust pan

6 eggs, separated

3/4 cup granulated sugar, divided

3/4 cup + 2 tablespoons unsweetened cocoa

2 1/2 teaspoons vanilla extract, divided

Pinch of salt

1 1/2 cups whipping cream

1/2 cup powdered sugar

Powdered sugar for garnish

Fresh berries for garnish

Preheat oven to 375°. Spray bottom and sides of 15x10 jelly-roll pan with cooking spray; line with wax paper. Spray wax paper; dust with cocoa. Set pan aside. Beat egg yolks at high speed with an electric mixer until foamy. Gradually add 1/4 cup granulated sugar, beating until thick and pale. Gradually stir in 3/4 cup cocoa, 1 1/2 teaspoons vanilla and salt. Beat until well blended. Beat egg whites until soft peaks form; gradually add remaining 1/2 cup granulated sugar, beating until stiff peaks form. Fold gently into cocoa mixture. Spread batter evenly into prepared jelly-roll pan. Bake 12-15 minutes or until a wooden pick inserted in center comes out clean. Sift remaining 2 tablespoons cocoa onto a clean, non-terry cloth towel, in a 15x10 rectangle shape. Remove cake from oven, run knife around edges to loosen. Turn cake out onto prepared towel. Peel wax paper off cake; trim cake edges, discard. Starting at a short end, roll cake and towel together. Place seam side down on wire rack to cool. To prepare filling, beat whipping cream at low speed with electric mixer until foamy; add powdered sugar and 1 teaspoon vanilla. Beat at high speed until soft peaks form. Unroll cake; spread evenly with whipped cream mixture, leaving a 1-inch border around edges. Reroll cake without towel. Place seam side down on serving platter; garnish if desired.

Serves 8

DAIRY

Marion Varon

Passover Truffle Cake

3 cups semisweet chocolate chips

1 cup unsalted butter

6 large eggs, at room temperature

Powdered sugar, cocoa and/or cinnamon sugar, if desired

Preheat oven to 425°. Coat 8-inch round cake pan with cooking spray. Line bottom with wax paper; spray paper with cooking spray. In saucepan, melt chocolate chips and butter over low heat; stir until well blended. In large bowl, beat eggs with electric mixer on high 7 minutes or until tripled and soft peaks form. Fold in chocolate mixture until blended. Pour into cake pan. Cover pan loosely with foil. Place a large roasting pan in oven; place cake pan inside. Pour boiling water into roasting pan to halfway up side of cake pan. Bake 40 minutes. Cake will look soft but set when cold. Cool cake in pan on wire rack. Cover; refrigerate 3 hours, or until firm. Invert on serving platter; shake down sharply to release cake. Peel off paper. If desired, garnish with powdered sugar, cocoa, and/or cinnamon sugar.

It is dense and rich. Cut into very small slices.

Serves 18

DAIRY

Marion Varon

Twelve-Egg Passover Cake

12 large eggs, separated

1½ cups sugar

1 lemon, zested

½ cup orange juice

1 cup cake meal, sifted

½ cup potato starch, sifted

1 quart strawberries

Sugar or sweetener to taste

1 cup whipping cream or 16 ounces frozen whipped topping, thawed

Preheat oven to 350°. Beat egg whites until stiff peaks form; set aside. Beat egg yolks and sugar until creamy. Add lemon zest and orange juice. Add cake meal and potato starch; mix until well blended. Fold in egg whites. Pour batter into tube pan. Bake 1 hour. Cool in pan on wire rack. To remove from pan, run knife or flexible metal spatula around edge of pan and around center post to loosen. Invert on wire rack; tap bottom of pan. Set aside. Wash strawberries. Set aside ½ of berries. Remove stems from remaining berries; cut into small pieces. Toss with sugar. Split cake into 2 layers. Top bottom half of cake with strawberries and sugar mixture. Put top layer in place. Beat whipping cream or thaw whipped topping. Ice entire cake. Use remaining strawberries to decorate top of cake.

Serves 12 to 16

DAIRY   Sadye H. Weill

Passover Cookies

2	eggs	2	cups ground pecans
1¹/₂	cups sugar	¹/₂	cup cake meal
¹/₄	teaspoon vanilla		Dash of salt

Preheat oven to 325°. Beat eggs and sugar until light and thick. Fold in vanilla, pecans, cake meal and salt. Drop by teaspoonful on baking pan lined with parchment paper. Bake 20 minutes.

PARVE   *Corinne F. Capilouto*

Passover Chocolate Chip Nut Cookies

2	cups matzah meal	1	teaspoon cinnamon
2	cups matzah farfel	¹/₂	teaspoon salt
1¹/₂	cups sugar	4	eggs
1	cup chocolate chips	²/₃	cup oil
1	cup nuts		

Preheat oven to 350°. Combine matzah meal, farfel, sugar, chocolate chips, nuts, cinnamon and salt. Make a well in middle of dry ingredients. Add eggs and oil into dry ingredients; mix well. Make into tablespoon size balls; flatten on greased cookie sheet. Bake 30 minutes.

Makes 24 cookies

PARVE   *Marsha Orange*

Lemon Cheesecake Bars

1½ cups soft coconut macaroon
    cookie crumbs
2 tablespoons melted margarine
2 (8 ounce) packages cream
    cheese, softened

½ cup sugar
1 teaspoon lemon zest
2½ tablespoons lemon juice
1 teaspoon vanilla extract
2 eggs

Preheat oven to 350°. Line bottom of 8-inch square baking pan with foil,
extending over sides of pan; spray with cooking spray. Mix cookie crumbs and
margarine; press into bottom of pan. In a bowl, beat cream cheese, sugar, zest,
juice and vanilla until well blended. Add eggs one at a time, mixing after each
just until blended. Pour over crumbs. Bake 20-25 minutes until center is almost
set and getting a little brown. Refrigerate 3 hours. Use foil handles to remove
cake from pan. Cut into bars.

An easy recipe with delicious results.

DAIRY
        Susan Bruchis

Emily's Passover Pecan Pralines

1 cup butter
1 cup brown sugar
1 cup chopped pecans

1 teaspoon vanilla
Matzah sheets

Preheat oven to 350°. Melt butter and brown sugar in saucepan until boiling.
Add pecans and vanilla; set aside. Lay sheets of matzah, side by side on jelly-
roll pan. Do not overlap sheets. Pour brown sugar mixture over matzah. Bake
10 minutes. Cool 15 minutes. Cut into squares. When cool, break squares;
store in air-tight container.

DAIRY
        Sylvia Capouano